4-3-2-1
LEADERSHIP

★ ★

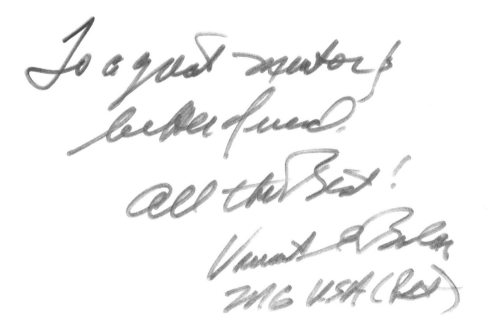

*"You want to be a better leader? Read this book.
It will inspire you, it will motivate you and you will learn
what General Boles has lived for 33 years in the military
and now as he brings his message to us 'civilians.' People matter,
you matter, and leaders make people better. This book is a
great investment in you, your people and your life."*

- Chester Elton, New York Times Bestselling
Author of *All In* and *The Carrot Principle*

*"At last! Major General Vincent E. Boles has taken the
powerful message he delivers in speeches and put it in a book for
all to read. 4-3-2-1 Leadership will inspire readers to action
with simple yet powerful principles that are battle tested."*

- Tony D'Amelio, CEO and Founder,
The D'Amelio Network

*"The concepts of teamwork and leadership don't change,
no matter if you are involved in a business team, the military,
or a sports team. General Vincent Boles understands and does
a great job of explaining the key factors that influence the
functioning of your team. This book allows you to learn
what took General Boles years of experience to gather
as he rose through the ranks of the U.S. Army."*

- Karl Mecklenburg, Speaker and NFL All Pro

"Major General Boles is one of those rare human beings who is able to entertain while educating. He has translated his experience of serving our country into a dynamic and accessible model of leadership. He is a role model for the ages (and he didn't even pay me to say this)!"

- Wendy Liebman, Comedienne,
Host of Showtime Special, *Taller on TV*

"4-3-2-1 Leadership has a message worth sharing, from a leader who is articulate, coherent and passionate, and has been tested in our toughest crucible and passed that test with flying colors."

- Mike Abrashoff, Captain, United States Navy (Retired)
Bestselling Author of *It's Your Ship*

"Vinny Boles' military experience as it relates to leadership in life and business is as unique as the man himself. Learn from one of our elite leaders in a profound and inspiring book that will surely change your perspective and give you tools for success."

- Mikki Williams, CSP, Professional Speaker,
Vistage Chair, *Mensch*, and Vinny's Mentor

"General Boles' 4-3-2-1 Leadership message aligned so closely with our Penn Mutual values of: Acting with Integrity; Respecting one another; Focusing on relationships; Sustaining our legacy and evoking a shared sense of belonging. I'm confident it will assist you on your leadership journey."

- Eileen McDonnell, CEO, Penn Mutual

"General Boles provides actionable tools you can use now to become a better leader. As a provider of in-person events, we hear a lot of presentations, but no one has ever received the accolades General Boles received during his presentations. I'm proud to live in a country where leaders like General Boles are leading our young men and women when they go into harm's way. After reading this book you will follow General Boles into battle as well, and he'll provide you the information that will make others want to likewise follow you."'

- John Kelly, CEO, Bluegrass Business Media

"Two-Star General Vincent E. Boles has faced extraordinary tests of leadership during his 33-year career within the U.S. Army, particularly while overseeing complex supply chain logistics during Operation Iraqi Freedom. He faced those challenges with an entrepreneurial mindset and can-do spirit. He relays the lessons he learned during his tenure as General with charisma and a dose of humor, calling it like it is."

— Mary Mazzio, CEO of 50 Eggs Films

4-3-2-1 Leadership
Lessons America's Sons and Daughters Taught Me
on the Road from Second Lieutenant to Two-Star General
Copyright © 2013 Vincent E. Boles, *www.vincentboles.com*

Published by:
Blooming Twig Books
New York / Tulsa
www.bloomingtwig.com

Cover design by Natasha Caine
Front cover photograph by Davin Grau/The Design Works, Inc.

Hardcover: ISBN 978-1-61343-034-7
eBook: ISBN 978-1-61343-035-4

First Edition

Printed in the United States of America.

Dedication

So many did so much to enable my success to occur.
One person, however, has been there for it all.
From deciding to start on this path of Army leadership,
committing to it as a career choice and finally to
ending it on our terms, Cheryl has been the
foundation for all the good that has come our way.
When I left an assignment, I had more than one
boss say, "We are going to miss you Vinnie,
but we are really sad to see Cheryl go."
For every life she has touched and made
better along the way (including mine),
this book is dedicated to Cheryl.

4-3-2-1
LEADERSHIP

Lessons America's Sons and Daughters Taught Me on
the Road from Second Lieutenant to Two-Star General

☆ ☆

Vincent E. Boles
Major General U.S. Army (Ret.)

Blooming Twig Books
New York / Tulsa

Table of Contents

FOREWORD

I have always known Major General Vincent E. Boles as "Vinny"—ever since the first day I met him. I congratulated him on receiving his first star, and when I addressed him as "General," his reply was, "I'm a servant to the people of the United States. You pay taxes, and taxes pay my salary, so I work for you—call me 'Vinny'." I knew I liked this man immediately!

As you read this book, or have the privilege to hear Vinny speak, you will certainly see and begin to understand how confident, competent, knowledgeable, capable, and experienced he really is. But Vinny is much more than that. He is also honest, caring, trusting, respectful, understanding, and supportive. In other words, he has all the traits and qualities that make him not only an outstanding leader, but a good and decent human being. Vinny is the real deal!

Vinny the Person

Having known Vinny for many years, he is not just a close friend, but actually more like family to my husband Ron and me. I love his wife, Cheryl, like a sister, as she spent a great deal of time with us when Vinny was deployed. Let me begin by describing the Vinny I know.

Vinny is the eldest son of Irish immigrants—a first generation American. His family carries the love and humor of a true Irish family. He was active in sports, respecting his coaches all of his life. He grew up in the heart of the

Big Apple—a true New Yorker in many ways. His colorful mannerisms and ways are a true asset to who he is.

Vinny is a loving and devoted husband to Cheryl, always attributing much of his success to her love and support. He is a devoted friend and just a pleasure to be around—always there for you and delighted to be so. He is, by far, one of the happiest people I know. He lives by his common saying: "Don't let anyone steal your joy." Be happy!

Vinny the Leader, Learner, and Teacher

Vinny doesn't *demand* respect; he *earns* it by his words and actions. He is a pleasure to be around, putting everyone at ease. He values opinions and suggestions, while making each person feel important. He truly embodies the concept of teamwork.

Vinny is both an active observer and a listener, and his desire to continually learn and build upon new ideas is evident. I shared a story with him about a roofing accident during my time as principal of an elementary school in Chambersburg, Pennsylvania. It involved a terrible situation that caused injuries to students while attending an assembly in the gymnasium. Part of the roof collapsed onto the children while contractors were working, making our school look like a war zone.

Vinny was keenly interested in how I had responded in this crisis, asking many questions. At the end of the conversation, he asked me, "What did you learn?" I was taken aback and quite honored when Vinny later asked me (a civilian) to relate my experiences as a leader in this crisis to his subordinate commanders and leaders at his Commanders' Conference. Our mutual respect and bond began!

Vinny's work at my school in Bettendorf, Iowa will never be forgotten. He has made a lifelong impression upon students, faculty, and parents. His desire to teach, to share, to guide was always evident. He asked me, "Do you think I can teach, Barbara?" The answer was an enthusiastic, "Yes! You've got it Vinny! You are a natural, and all are privileged to be touched by your presence and spirit."

Vinny the Author

Vinny loves his family and friends. Vinny loves people. Vinny loves life! Vinny found it exciting to be a Soldier, and being a Soldier was his passion.

Vinny knows what he is writing about and sharing with you—the reader. He's been there, and is highly successful and continues to be so. As an illustration of that, one of his favorite sayings is, "Hey! I'm workin' here!"

Believe him…he is.

I'm absolutely confident that by applying the insights and concepts gained and refined over the many years of Vinny Boles' experience will make you a better leader, learner, listener, and teacher in all of life's endeavors.

I am proud and honored to be a part of his lifelong journey.

Enjoy!!!

Barbara Herter was born in Johnstown, Pennsylvania, and has been a career educator and principal in both Pennsylvania and Iowa. She received her B.S. in Elementary Education from the University of Pittsburgh, and her Master's degree in Early Childhood Education from Shippensburg Unviersity. She is currently the principal of Our Lady of Lourdes Grammar School in Bettendorf, Iowa.

She has been married to her husband, Ronald Herter—a career US Army Civil Servant—for 41 years. They first met Vinny Boles in 2001 when he assumed command of the US Army's Field Support Command in Rock Island, Illinois—Ron served as his deputy. This professional relationship blossomed as the Herters and the Boles grappled with the stress of responding to the events of 9-11, as well as Vinny's subsequent deployment for the invasion of Iraq in 2003. Barbara's children at Lourdes "adopted" the Boles, and the love keeps on coming!

Joining the Army, May 23, 1976.

PREFACE

In 2009, I retired after more than 33 years in the United States Army. My journey began in 1976 as a 21-year-old Second Lieutenant, with no idea what lay ahead. My success was not pre-ordained; no one knew that I would retire more than three decades later as a Two-Star General. I certainly never would have guessed that, after retirement, I would be traveling the country giving talks on leadership, consulting with companies on supply chain optimization, and teaching logistics as an adjunct professor.

As a young man, all I knew was that I did not want to spend the rest of my life mopping floors and tending bar in Boles's Bar and Restaurant at 5th Avenue and 39th Street in Manhattan. When my father turned to me one day when I was in my mid-teens and said, "Some day, this will all be yours," I knew I needed to get "Plan B."

The Army emerged as my Plan B, and a Reserve Officer Training Corps (ROTC) scholarship to pay for my last two years in college convinced me that the four years I would have to commit to the Army were four years I would be away from mopping floors. Simply stated, I had no visions of grandeur; I joined the Army to run away from what I did not want to do.

I can't say the exact moment I stopped running away, and started embracing my new profession and life. I was blessed to have a long and interesting career, and I learned every leadership lesson along that road from America's sons and daughters. Now that I have given more than a hundred talks on leadership around the nation and the world, I have come to believe that those lessons can be applied to any organization.

Although my experiences in leadership come from the military, this is not a book exclusively about leadership in the United States Army; it is a book about leadership in any organization—in *your* organization.

★ ☆

Every year, we bring 170,000 new people into the United States Army, and they come from all walks of life, all economic backgrounds, all races, and both genders. We bring all these individuals into an entity, get them working together, and make them part of a 1.1-million-person operation that runs very, very well. The nation expects and deserves no less. The Army continues to be one of the most effective organizations in training leaders out of necessity. We *need* them.

Those who train for leadership in the Army also need effective and practical techniques. I learned this lesson in 2004, after my first deployment to Iraq. As Commanding General for the Army's training center for Ordnance Soldiers, I worried that all my efforts would concentrate on the technical training needed by the Army's 120,000 Ordnance Soldiers. These Ordnance Soldiers are responsible for a range of missions, from ground and electronic maintenance, to all ammunition handling, to the disarming of explosives such as IEDs (improvised explosive devices). I could not have been more wrong; I found that the Soldiers I was responsible for training were fully adept at performing the technical aspects of their duties. Our conversations focused instead on leadership and the challenges of leading during a time of war.

Officers would ask me, "Sir, how do I lead a team when I am in Fort Hood, Texas, and the team is currently in Fort Polk, Louisiana, and the first time I'm ever going to meet them is on a battlefield in Iraq?"

The Officers also confided in me and asked me for my opinion on what they should do next: "I don't know how to connect with my team," or "I don't have much time, but I have to get a team together quickly, and then some-how merge them with a team that is already in battle."

As I addressed every class of Officers (from Second Lieutenants to Colonels) who came through that training center in those 26 months, more than anything else, those Officers wanted help in how to lead their teams more effectively.

From my earliest days in the Army, I have been intrigued by the connection that effective leaders establish with those they lead. Those leaders are able to move our country, our cause, our mission, and our people onward and upward. Again and again, at every level, I have seen this leadership emerge as the "secret sauce"—the ingredient that has made the difference in both success and failure.

I have observed teams that were given every possible benefit to ensure success: resources, people, time, and attention. Yet when leadership was lacking, those teams consistently failed.

On the flip side, I have observed teams that were short of every resource except inspired leadership. I saw those teams thrive time and time again.

Over the 33 years I served, without fail, when I didn't know the answer, I would look around at the members of my team, and I would find it. The answer was always provided to me in the form of a smiling Soldier. America's sons and daughters have been my touchstone, again and again.

Several years ago, a Colonel who worked with me when she was a Captain, came to my office in the Pentagon and said, "Sir, I understand you're retiring."

I said, "Yes."

She said, "Well, when are you going to write your book? Because I've been using your leadership lessons for years—when I taught at West Point, and ever since then."

That was the first time I thought about writing this book. I didn't take the notion too seriously until I started doing more public speaking, at which point I began getting this question more and more often.

After a speech in New York City, a gentleman put up his hand and said, "I don't know what your plans are, but I'd buy this book if you'd write it." That was one of my favorite encouragements, and I've had many. Thank you to everyone who put in a good word with me—because you are now reading my first book. I truly hope that you find some value between these covers, and that I am not simply waxing philosophically, but that you can really benefit from these tools that I have picked up from, and used with, America's sons and daughters along this journey.

☆ ☆

I am not a motivational speaker.

I take great pains to avoid that title because I find that motivational speakers are like seagulls on the beach. They fly around, they swoop down, they make a little noise, they take your money, drop some "leadership fairy dust," and leave. What I find is that fairy dust doesn't last very long, and I don't want to be one of those speakers.

I want to be a speaker that runs into someone from the audience a year later, and that person says, "I'm still using the stuff you shared."

I've encountered others who say, "We're still using that tool you gave us to end meetings effectively. It still works. You were exactly right." This feedback is incredibly rewarding to me, and this kind of impact remains the goal of my public speaking work.

Instead of "motivational speaker," I would like to say that I'm a speaker who has been molded by the toughest crucible: leading American men and women into active combat. Let it suffice to say, I'm not a speaker who's going to talk about fairy dust and motivation. I didn't just read a book about leadership and have a couple of ideas. The guidelines in this book are truly what America's sons and daughters have taught me.

Another reason I wrote this book is to remember the Soldiers who bravely stand at the ready to defend our freedom and security. Those Soldiers have been my touchstone again and again; they have never faltered and never failed. We must never forget those Soldiers who have lost their lives, or those who have given a large portion of their lives to the greater good of their fellow citizens and our nation.

At the conclusion of my talks, and during my travels through airports and hotels, people often have come up to me and said, "Thank you for your service."

My response has always been, and will always be, immediate and heartfelt: "It's a great country to serve, and I got more from this country than I ever gave."

I am honored to share this journey with you.

Major General Vincent E. Boles (Retired), March 2013

Fort Knox, Kentucky, 1978 — Promotion to First Lieutenant.

April 1991 somewhere in Iraq soaking in the aftermath of the
100-Hour War (L-R: Vinny Boles, Lieutenant Colonel Steve Marshman,
Captain Lorraine Holland and Brigadier General Jerry Rutherford)

INTRODUCTION

*"So much of what we call management consists of
making it difficult for people to work."*

- Peter Drucker

I don't stand in front of the mirror and practice motivational speeches. Nothing I can say in an hour-long keynote presentation or write between the covers of this book will motivate you to be a better person. That motivation has to come from inside you. You have to decide that you want to show up and put your heart into what you are doing. In my case, putting my heart into what I was doing meant leading others.

All great leaders were at one time rookies. Fortunately, we can all learn leadership skills, especially if we have the desire and are willing to dedicate time and effort. However, the road from a rookie to great leader is often *hindered* by poor management.

Here is how I see it: leadership is very different from management. When I am *managing* something, I am looking at what has to get done, and it's impersonal and detached. When I am *leading*, it's personal; my heart has to be in it, because I'm forging a connection that lights a spark in others, and encourages them to be their *best* when accomplishing a task.

I don't want to give you any formulas or theories in this book. There are countless other books that fulfill that niche. Instead, by writing simple anecdotes and experiences from my own career leading America's sons and daughters, I hope to encourage you to think about all of the *possibilities*, and help you to be the best leader you can be.

This book is a collection of the tools, tactics, techniques, and procedures you can use in your leadership practice to better your team and your business. I learned these lessons over 33 years in the service of this great country. My sincere wish is that these tools will help you as they have helped me.

☆ ☆

My education has not been a solo trip. America's sons and daughters have been the teammates who helped me to develop and refine these tools, and they are *really* great teammates. Their fingerprints are all over every ribbon I have and every star I have been privileged to wear.

I have heard many people through the years say, "I'm doing my best." But leadership is about progress and improvement. My best had to get better. I had to grow and develop in every assignment, at every rank. I had to demonstrate that I improved. The ten 4-3-2-1 Leadership tools I present in this book are designed to help you ensure that *your* best gets better, and that your *team's* best gets better.

Along my journey, I have learned that leadership is not about *me*. If you are a leader, or aspire to be a leader, remember that leadership is not about *you*, either. Leadership is about how you meet your *team's* needs, how you provide an environment where they can flourish, and how everyone's best can get better. It's about *them*.

Four Expectations People Have of Their Leaders

I begin this book with those who are most important—those who are being led—and discuss the four expectations they have of their leaders. Teams expect their leader to establish structure, manage relationships, balance risk, and make decisions. These four expectations are critical because in order to get every team member's commitment to the organization, a leader must acknowledge their expectations.

As a leader, listening to and understanding your team's expectations will enable you to meet them at their level, and build a full toolkit to handle any situation that might arise. If your only leadership tool is your own, individual perspective, all you have is a hammer, and every leadership problem you will encounter had better look like a nail.

Whenever I had a leadership challenge connecting with someone, it was usually because I approached that challenge from my perspective and started with the comment, "You don't understand."

Then I realized that maybe *I* was the one who didn't understand. There's an old saying that rings true in this case: *When you point a finger at somebody, there are still four fingers pointing back at you.*

In other words, I was approaching the situation with my hammer, when I needed to pull out my entire toolkit and see what might work in the given situation. I begin this book with these four expectations because understanding them has been critical for me as a leader, in every situation from war to interpersonal relationships.

Three Critical Questions a Leader Must Ask and Answer

As a leader, you need to develop a cohesive alignment between what you want your people to do and their understanding of their responsibilities. The next section of the book discusses the three critical questions a leader must ask and answer: What's the standard? What's the system? Who's in charge?

If I could tell my people, "Here's what I want you to do in terms of a standard, I've ensured you have a system to accomplish that standard, and I know who is in charge of each component," things would almost always work out. And whenever something went wrong personally, professionally, or in a unit I was responsible for, it was because I didn't ask and answer those three questions; people would waste a lot of time and energy trying to figure out the answers I might have given.

A leader's job is to clarify, not obscure. When I would tell people to do something, I made sure that what they had to do was clear to them. If, when I am done explaining the task, I see a blank look on their faces, I have not done my job properly. I shouldn't get, "Hunh?" I should get, "Got it!"

An effective leader also responds to questions by offering clear answers, not by saying, "I gave you all I got, and if you can't figure things out, that's too bad."

Two Reasons for Stress in an Organization

Once you've identified your people's expectations and then given them standards, systems, and clear responsibilities, your people are ready to launch.

However, when they take on their tasks, there will be friction points, which occur during any interaction. One of a leader's critical jobs is to identify and lubricate those friction points, which fall into two groups: either the leader knows something his or her people don't know, or the people know something the leader doesn't know. Those are the two reasons for stress in an organization.

This lack of communication is not difficult to see, and it's not complicated to remedy. When a leader sees stress in an organization, they tend to pull back when what they need to do is push forward, communicating effectively and more often.

One Non-Negotiable — Trust

The most critical component in any organization is trust. How can a leader best engender and establish trust between him- or herself and those being led? Trust can be reinforced every day, or it can be diminished every day.

In combat, trust is crucial. At times, I had to tell America's sons and daughters, "You go out that gate, and you operate out there in the face of any enemy that's going to try and kill you."

When I wanted these national treasures, these Soldiers to do that, they weren't going to do it because they *liked* me, because they *respected* me, or because they thought I was a *nice guy.* They did it because they thought, "I trust him."

I had the greatest honor of any leader. America's sons and daughters put their trust in me. They trusted that I had established a structure, managed a relationship, balanced risk, and made the right decisions. They trusted that I had given them a standard, identified systems, understood what they were in charge of, and made sure that they understood the same thing. I gave everything I had to manage those stress points, and alleviated the friction as best I could. We succeeded together as a team because they trusted me, and I worked hard to earn that trust.

Every day, people look at their leaders and ask, "Is this leader worthy of my trust and confidence?" And you might look at me and say, "All of these tools roll off your tongue very nicely, and sound good in theory. But how do you really build trust in an organization?"

I have seen this work in all kinds of organizations, and I truly believe that understanding the four expectations your people have of you, asking and answering the three questions, and understanding the two causes of stress, will help build and engender the trust in your leadership, and in your organization.

How to Get the Most Out of This Book

If you picked up this book, then you are probably interested in becoming a leader or improving your current leadership skills. You can use this book for your own internal professional development by reading through, making some notes, and saying, "Here are some ways I want to start doing things." You can also focus on your areas of interest and pick and choose the chapters you prefer to read.

This book can also be used as a professional development tool for your staff and the various leaders in your organization. In the body of the book, I include ten takeaways at the end of each chapter. These takeaways list the crucial points of each chapter.

If one of those takeaways intrigues you, you can turn to the relevant section of the chapter and read more. These takeaways can also function as an evaluation tool for your team. After each takeaway, you can ask yourself and your team, "How well are we doing on this?" Evaluate yourself and your team and then re-visit these takeaways to see how you've improved.

Your team can also come together and discuss each chapter without focusing exclusively on the takeaways. Here are a couple of examples:

When your team reads about the four expectations people have of their leaders, a note-taker in the meeting can record your team's response to the following questions: "How well are we doing on these four expectations, and what are some of the things we can do to better meet these expectations?"

In the section on the three questions to ask and answer, you could evaluate your organization by asking your team, "How are we doing with these three questions? What are our standards? What are our systems? Who's in charge? How well are we doing in all three areas?"

In the Conclusion, I have included the ten questions I am most often asked following my talks. In Thoughts to Leave You With and the Afterword, I add some final thoughts on balance, attitude, and bringing your team together.

4 -3 -2 -1
LEADERSHIP

FOUR EXPECTATIONS
Teams Have of Leaders

""If we can support President [George W.] Bush
as he does the four critical things he has to do
to meet this crisis, America will be fine.
America will get through this."

- Former President Bill Clinton,
September 2001

I had just arrived in my office on the Rock Island Arsenal in Illinois when I saw a group of my team members gathered around, looking at a TV. The date was September 11, 2001 and it was eight in the morning (Central time). They all knew that I was born in New York City, and they asked me, "What does it mean, Sir, when a plane hits the World Trade Center?"

The intensity of that question didn't hit me immediately—I thought this was one of those cases where a small plane would veer off its path and hit a building on a foggy day. I gave my "informed New Yorker" view of the situation, saying, "That kind of thing is very rare, but it's not unheard of, and well, sometimes stuff happens."

I didn't know that it was a crystal clear day in New York City. I also didn't know that this wasn't a small plane, but a 747, and there were three more planes that would change the course of American history.

In late July 2001, I started my first command position as a General Officer; I was officially the Commanding General of the US Army's Field Support Command (FSC). Though its headquarters was located at Rock Island, the FSC's reach was global—anywhere the Army had Soldiers' boots on the ground.

At the FSC, we had three primary missions:

1. Care for all the War Reserve Equipment located around the world and, on order, issue it out for combat operations.

2. Operate 52 Logistics Assistance Offices, providing all manner of assistance, from technical experts in Army Equipment and Systems to ensuring that units maintained their readiness level. Also, these people served as "systems scouts," letting the Army Logistics Enterprise know about systemic problems units had with equipment, hopefully catching those problems early.

3. Plan for and utilize the Army's Logistics Civilian Augmentation Program (LOGCAP). In this relatively new program, the Army would use civilian contractors to augment Logistical Operations (they were being used in the Balkans, and in 2001, were also operating a small contract for housing and life support for forces in East Timor).

Even though FSC was only two years old, it already gained the reputation, due to the depth and breadth of its mission set, of being a challenging command to get your head into and your arms around. An additional hurdle was that because FSC was so new, there were varying expectations about its usefulness. To some, it was the next cure for cancer, HIV, and heart disease, all rolled into one. To others, it was just another organizational redesign so that the post-Cold War Army could fair-share the resource shortfalls that came with the "Peace Dividend" of the 1990's. My experience told me that reality was somewhere in between these two, but a large part of my job would involve managing these expectations.

My new responsibilities would mostly entail traveling around the world to different bases, working to fair-share any shortages at those locations, making sure that the Army was spending its resources on the most critical opportunities and taking appropriate risks to mitigate these resource shortages.

As I watched Washington D.C. fade in the rearview mirror and headed to the heartland of America, I had no inkling that any kind of major wartime initiative would ignite later that year. After the fall of the Soviet Union and a hundred-hour victory during the Desert Storm campaign, the common thought was that it was doubtful any other major war or operation would surface anytime soon.

☆ ☆

On September 11, 2001, a new reality intruded, and with it, my job description and our unit's mission changed. On 9/11, an entity with no standing military, no economy or government structure attacked the United States of America, and killed over 3,000 people. In the aftermath of the first attack on American soil in 60 years, the FSC team's role immediately changed from planning for a contingency (what might happen, and we hadn't planned for this) to one where we would be actively engaged in supporting combat operations. The challenge ahead was how our team would operate in this critical transition period where the stakes were high, the pressure was on, and the outcome was uncertain.

Leaders have to set the conditions for a successful transition well in advance of it breaking upon them. In such new circumstances, I wasn't able to simply go out and hire a new team that was ready for support operations during wartime. I would need to focus our existing team as it transitioned from contingency to action.

I couldn't go out the door and say, "Okay, give me the team that's going to execute this mission since these people already planned everything." Instead, I had to turn to my people and say, "It is your job to plan the operation. Now it's also your job to execute it."

In the coming hours and days, my FSC teammates on Rock Island and around the world revealed themselves to be national treasures. General

George C. Marshall (the Army's Chief of Staff during World War II) described his experience in WWII after the Pearl Harbor attack by saying, "When I had time, [before the Pearl Harbor attack] I had no money. Now I have all the money I need but no time." This perfectly describes the enormity of the challenge my FSC teammates and I faced after 9/11.

My people understood what needed to be done, and how to do it. They were besieged (but not defeated) by multiple and seemingly endless requests for information: "How much money and how fast can you fix 250 of x and 350 of y and get them to Kuwait, Afghanistan, the Horn of Africa or anywhere else?"

They went from normal workdays of eight hours, five days a week to three shifts a day, around the clock, seven days a week. Even as I write this, eleven years after the 9/11 attacks, they are still working towards that common goal of supporting the force.

A few days after the 9/11 attacks, I found myself watching the C-Span television network. I heard former President Bill Clinton speak to a group in New York City. He said there were four critical things that President Bush would have to execute in order to meet the challenge that 9/11 had brought us, and it was critical for the nation to support him. According to President Clinton, President Bush would need to do the following four things.

1.   Establish structure

2.   Manage relationships

3.   Balance risk

4.   Make decisions

Those four simple yet direct insights resonated with me, and I immediately wrote them down. I didn't yet realize that I would use those four tasks as a guidepost in leading my team during a time of war.

Throughout the next eight years as a General Officer, my success or failure, time and time again, traced itself directly back to one of these four critical insights.

1ST EXPECTATION
Establish Structure

*"Organization charts and fancy titles
count for next to nothing."*

- General Colin Powell (Retired)

Walter Reed Army Medical Center—Spring 2008

Leadership is personal. You have to be committed—really committed—to do it well. You have to connect with people, take the time to get to know them, and determine what leadership tool works best with them in order to fully engage them in the accomplishment of a group aim. Put another way, they have to get to *know* you, before they *trust* you. If they don't get to know you, you will simply be managing the accomplishment of tasks, not truly leading them.

After 32 years, I thought that lesson had been fully ingrained in my Leadership Brain Housing Group (AKA my mind). However, on this day, I was reacquainted with this lesson in a manner I won't ever forget.

I had just finished a medical appointment at Walter Reed (nothing critical, just "old man" aches and pains that we can't shake off after 50 like we did when we were 30), and I asked the staff at Walter Reed to let me visit with the wounded Soldiers who were there from Iraq and Afghanistan.

Many other Soldiers and Officers similarly make and take the time to visit these Warriors at Walter Reed and Bethesda every day, so my visit wasn't difficult for them to manage. The staff was great at this, knowing what patients wanted to be seen and those who valued their privacy. My wife, Cheryl, was with me, and she has background as a nurse, which did a lot to ease the tension in the room as well.

We entered a room where the patient was a young Lieutenant about 25 or 26 years old. His father was at the Soldier's bedside, and I asked him the usual questions.

"Where are you from, Sir?" I asked the father.

"Phoenix. I'm retired," he responded.

"How is he doing?"

"It's tough."

"What are you doing now that you're retired, Sir?"

"I'm taking care of my son," he said to me, as he pointed to his boy with quiet determination.

At this point, the young Lieutenant started to pay attention, and I got to see how "tough" the situation really was. He had lost both legs above the knee, and he had lost his right arm at the shoulder. His left arm was encased in some kind of metal cage from the elbow to his fingertips, and it was in traction.

The brave young man smiled at me and said, "Good morning, Sir," and we began to talk, falling into that rhythm of conversation between Soldiers since the Roman Legions. We spoke about his unit, his location in combat, and a few comments about equipment. We moved on to our marital status—he was married, and there were pictures on his wall of family, friends, and a massive and very happy Labrador retriever.

Next, I explained that my job in the Army involved supplies and equipment, I asked how his injuries had occurred, and if we could make anything we had issued better.

He told me he had been in the front passenger seat of an up-armored HMMWV ("Humvee"), when an IED (Improvised Explosive Device) went off, and he had suffered the wounds I saw in front of me. Thanks to great medical intervention immediately following his injuries, he had been able to survive the incident. Three other Soldiers from his unit in the vehicle had been killed.

During our talk, his mother joined us. The Lieutenant looked at his parents, and with a friendly toss of his head, asked them to leave the room. Cheryl followed.

The young man asked me to come to his bedside, and then he beckoned me even closer. I had my ear to his cheek when he said, "Sir, would you please scratch my nose?"

As I did, he thanked me, and I was convinced I had just accomplished the most important task of the week.

Then he looked at me and said with a seriousness only a survivor can understand, "I failed, Sir. I didn't bring my guys back. I'm the only one who lived."

With all he had suffered already, and would suffer in the days, months, and years ahead, this leader, more than 25 years my junior, affirmed something that day. He was committed to be a leader who was connected to his Soldiers, and even after their deaths, he was still connected to them.

I listened as he talked about them, as he told me what he loved about them, and as he spoke of what he missed about them. Then, he asked me, "What do I do now, Sir?"

I didn't only hear the words he spoke in that moment. I also knew what he was saying beneath those words. He was asking me, "How do I go on?"

The two stars on my uniform, and my years of experience in the Army, had helped me in many situations, but they didn't help me answer this brave Soldier's question.

I answered him the only way I knew how. I spoke from my heart, and my experience. I told him that he had been saved for a reason, and that a combination of luck, faith, and certain equipment, worn in a certain way, had spared his life. Now he had to dedicate himself to finding answers to the question, "Why?" Then he could chart his course into the future, ensuring that it would be a path that would honor the service and sacrifice of those Soldiers in his charge who had not returned.

He thanked me, we hugged, and then I scratched his nose again.

As I departed, his dad and mom thanked me for my time.

On the drive out of Walter Reed, I realized this young man—this young national treasure—had given me more than I could ever give him.

Saying, "leadership is personal," sounds great as it rolls off your tongue. But it really hits you when you see someone who lives that principle.

Leadership and success are not ultimately about rank and titles. Rank and titles can enable you to get something done, but true success originates with your identity as a person, and how you lead. What ultimately emerges from that will demonstrate your ability to establish a leadership structure in a manner that benefits the team for which you are responsible.

In this chapter, we will divide the structures that leaders employ into two groups: 1. Internal Wiring, and 2. External Wiring. Internal Wiring is all about whether leaders use their head, their heart, or a combination of the two, when making decisions. External Wiring is about the importance of wall charts to leadership decisions.

Internal Wiring

As anyone who has taken a Myers Briggs Temperament Indicator (MBTI) knows, we all have certain predispositions. Some of us are introverted, and some are extroverted. I might be a feeling person, and you might be a sensing person. In any case, the MBTI helps us to identify how we are structured emotionally, and how we, in turn, have a tendency to function in the world around us.

When I give talks in front of various organizations, I always ask, "How many of you have had a boss, supervisor, or leader who just doesn't know how to tell you what they want?" A good portion of the heads in the room nod along with me, so I continue: "You think to yourself, *I'd be happy to give them what they want, if I just knew what it was!*" In all the years I have said this line, it never fails to get a great reaction from the audience.

What it comes down to is that, oftentimes, people just don't understand their leaders because they might be wired differently. If that is the situation, it falls to the leader to understand that difference, and to work on closing that critical gap of understanding.

There are many kinds of leaders. Some are data-driven. They crave statistical data analysis. Other leaders just want a quick summary. When I put a 300-page report in their hands, they say, "Vinny, give me the five critical points here on a one-page fact sheet." Still others say, "Give me this 300-page report as well as an executive summary, and then I will read both, grade your homework, and see how well you did." I will leave it to your imagination how much fun that experience was.

Where do you fall in the spectrum of leadership?

Are you a leader who is data-driven, who needs statistical analysis before you make a decision? Do you look at trends and data from the last three fiscal years before you make a decision? You probably make decisions with your head before your heart.

Or are you alternatively a leader who prefers to sit at the table, look at the information, and then think about the individuals on your team, processing what they will be comfortable with? Most likely, you try to make decisions with your heart before your head. "Go with my gut" best expresses your method.

Don't worry if you don't fit cleanly into one of these categories. The decision process is usually not an either-or; it's a complex combination of both. However, under the stress of time and budget, when leaders have to make decisions under stress, they will default to the style they are most comfortable operating within.

Rather than go into too many details about this, let me illustrate this point about the head and the heart with a little exercise I do with my audiences. Put this book down, and cross your arms over your chest.

Now that you have crossed your arms, let them relax, and notice how you feel in this position. I assume that you are probably comfortable, as just about all of us are, because we cross our arms routinely.

Now, take your arms and cross them the other way. If you had your right forearm on top, put your left forearm on top this time. Uncomfortable, isn't it? Not impossible, just not something you are normally "wired" to do.

If you are in a particularly difficult situation at work or home, with a boss or an employee, a spouse or relative, take a minute to stop and cross your arms, and you will remember that we are all wired differently.

From time to time, there would be a proposal to bring Soldiers in to work on the weekend for a special project or, as that famous maxim states, to "get ahead of the power curve" (in other words, "We're behind and can't catch up on a normal schedule"). Throughout my career I would observe this situation and saw that leaders had various ways of reacting to this extra work on the weekend. The following brief examples will illustrate the Internal Wiring of three different leaders.

Leader A would agree to the weekend hours but attempt to prepare in advance, saying, "Well, you have to give me six weeks' notice before you bring folks in on the weekend. If you can give me that much time, we will be able to adequately plan for it and make the best use of it."

In other words, those like Leader A would do whatever they could to avoid flying by the seat of their pants when the weekend in question arrived.

Leader A had a mostly "head" approach but was very reasonable, and also took the "heart" into consideration.

Leader B would say, "No, before we work on a weekend, I need to do a business case analysis. Tell me how much it will cost to bring all the troops in, turn all the lights on, turn on all the power, and get everything operational, and then show me what we will produce."

He or she would continue to ask questions, such as, "How many work orders will we close up? How many requisitions will we be able to fill? How much training will we make up?"

Leader B was an individual who was mostly driven by the "head" and very little by the "heart."

Leader C sees things a different way entirely, bringing the "heart" heavily into the mix.

I watched one time as a Soldier walked into a Commander's office with all possible statistical data, showing that weekend work would add a great deal of value. All of the data pointed logically towards the weekend workdays taking place.

This Commander, who had watched his Soldiers deployed for 12-15 months, knew how eager they were, and how critical it was for them to reconnect with their families, responded in a way the Soldier with the statistical data didn't expect. He said, "Wait a minute. I just drove through town before I came on post, and I saw that the Little League baseball signups are this weekend."

At first, the Soldier didn't know why the Commander would bring up Little League, but he kept listening. "We just caused Soldiers to be absent for last year's Little League signups because of their deployment, and it just wouldn't be right to make them miss another big event like this with their kids, so let's not bring them in this weekend."

None of the three leaders' styles are "wrong" ways to deal with an issue. However, in order have a well-performing team, members of a team need to know how their boss is "wired." And if you are the leader, you have to let your people know how you are wired. In the Army as well as any workplace, if employees and the boss understand how one another are wired, they can spend their energy making work more efficient and easy.

In summary, if *leaders* know how they are wired, and the *people* know how the leader is wired, the following three things will happen.

1. The people will be able to get information to the leader more quickly.

2. The people will process things for the leader more efficiently. They will be focused on what he/she needs, not what they wonder he/she *might* need. Leaders will find that when they ask three questions, their people will come back with five answers, because they have the time to think about the questions the leaders didn't ask but will need to know the answers to in the near future.

3. All office interactions will have more value.

External Wiring

External wiring diagrams, which map out your organization so that each member of your team can understand their role in the greater purpose of the organization, are very important to the effective collaboration of all levels of hierarchy. As effective as they are, these diagrams, also called wall charts, are perceived very differently by various members of your team, depending on their experience level and where they fit on the chart. I will describe the perspectives of both junior and senior leaders on such charts.

Junior leaders who are new to the organization are often inexperienced and have had very little opportunity to influence the external wiring diagram. But it doesn't take long for them to figure things out, and within a few hours or days, they see "who's who in the zoo."

If you are a junior leader, the following are a few tips for you as you initially review the wall chart.

- Look at the date on the copy. If it's not within the last year, it may not be very useful. Some organizations will redo their charts annually, either in conjunction with the fiscal year, whether it's April, July, October, or January, or they may do the chart in conjunction with the calendar year.

- Many organizations now will update the chart on a more routine basis and will keep it online—do some scouting and you will find it.

- Observe the individuals who occupy the CEO and COO suites. Learn their names and the names of their assistants. Pay special attention to their assistants. (Seems too simple? Trust me, it matters.)

- Pay attention to titles and departments. If Marketing, Financial, and HR heads are all vice presidents, and you see that the person in sales is listed as a Senior Vice President, or an Executive Vice President, that usually means in a debate or discussion, the senior will carry additional sway.

- Keep on the lookout for "special groups" in your organization. They might call themselves a "staff group," a "study group," an "initiatives group," or the "CEO's team." They might also have a completely different title that doesn't make sense at first, like "Snow White and the Seven Dwarves."

At the Pentagon, "Snow White and the Seven Dwarves" was a special group run by the Chief of Staff of the Army. They were not fairy-tale characters—far from it! "Snow White," rumor has it, was a white-haired, aging Colonel. The seven "dwarves" were seven experienced Lieutenant Colonels who performed well in the field for the Army and were believed to possess the potential for greater contributions to the Army and greater service.

If you had the opportunity to be a "dwarf," it was considered a developmental assignment, and many of the "dwarves" that I knew have since become General Officers in the Army. Being a "dwarf" gave these future General Officers an opportunity to work underneath a senior Colonel who operated for the Army Chief of Staff, handling significant issues, and getting to experience how things worked across the entire Army. For example, a "training dwarf" traveling with the Chief of Staff would get to observe training activities across the Army, not just at Fort X or Y.

At an early stage in my career, I had a chance to see the impact of "dwarves" firsthand. I was a First Lieutenant at Fort Knox, Kentucky, serving as a Maintenance Officer for a heavy maintenance company. Unbeknownst to me, one of the "dwarves" was visiting Fort Knox and knew my Battalion Commander (a Lieutenant Colonel). He decided to send the "dwarf" down so that I could give him a tour. The Battalion Commander informed my immediate boss (a Captain), but he simply told me, "A friend of the boss is coming. Give him a tour."

The "dwarf" arrived alone, and I took him around. He was very friendly and had an agenda. He also asked very detailed questions about techniques, challenges (in the post-Vietnam Army we had a number of them), and how we were coping. I just thought I was helping my boss.

About 30 minutes into the tour, my Lieutenant Colonel and Captain showed up, looking a bit concerned. I later discovered that they had a discussion and discovered I had not been rehearsed. They headed down to the shop area, and there the "dwarf" and I were having a discussion.

My bosses later asked me, "What exactly did you tell him?" I realized when I saw their concern that these "dwarves" were significant far beyond their rank in terms of influence. It must have worked out all right, because the "dwarf" later called my Battalion Commander, and said I had indeed been "most helpful."

If your organization has such a "special group," pay special attention to anything they ask for. They usually are not asking for themselves. I have seen more than one professional reputation self-destruct after either ignoring such people or not working well with them. On the other hand, I have seen people shine after positive productive interactions with this special group.

★ ☆

Senior leaders who have been with an organization for a long time have a completely different perspective on the external wiring diagram. Of course, they were around while the diagram took shape, so they are more familiar with it than junior leaders. But there are deeper differences.

Here are my observations over the last 35 years on what senior leaders do. They pay close attention to the organizational structure, and after a 60-120 day period of initial transition, they will initiate a process to modify it in tune with their experience and preferences (that process is often referred to as "just tweaking it"). Some will direct Legal to report directly to them or they will put Human Resources underneath the Chief Financial Officer, and they will call it Resource Management, and have HR report to them.

Additionally, I have observed that personalities weigh in on such adjustments. Specifically, if top managers like or don't like certain personnel interactions, they may bring the person in question closer or push that person further away. It's not normally "personal" but just a leader's predisposition to stay in their sweet spot, where they are comfortable. For example, if the CEO has an engineering background, they will be comfortable in that arena and gravitate to it. Likewise, if the CEO was developed in the financial arena, the demands of that will seem more familiar to them and thus perhaps easier.

The following two things are worthy of your consideration if you are a senior leader.

> 1. Understand the reasons behind the structure you have inherited before you attempt to change it.

To help you with this, there is usually a group of experienced old hands who will probably present the creation of this structure and can let you know what caused it. For example, one question you might ask would be, "Why does legal report directly to the CEO?"

The old hands might respond, "We had a sexual harassment complaint in the 1990's, so we split HR up, kept the VP separate from RM and we had legal report directly to the CEO because it was taking up a lot of his time."

> 2. Determine whether your motivation for the change in structure is masking a systemic problem in the organization.

Let me give you a hypothetical situation. Taking over as the CEO, you have been going around for 90-120 days having interactions with folks and learning how everything works in the organization.

Over time, you become increasingly uncomfortable in meetings with your Vice President of Marketing, named George. You are a thoughtful, deliberate person, and you are finding George is a bit more gregarious than you are, and presents a "fly-by-the-seat-of-his-pants" component of his personality that you are uncomfortable with.

You convince yourself (it didn't take a long conversation) that Marketing should now report to the VP of Sales. After all, selling generates the revenue that drives the business, and marketing reps have to generate sales, so you are doing what you can to forge a better relationship between Sales and Marketing.

Your inability to get along with VP George might arise from your observation of George's performance in juxtaposition with his personality. He might be using his gregarious attitude as a smoke screen for the fact that he has no marketing plan or strategy to develop a plan. You may instinctively know this, but for various reasons, you choose not to delve into the problem and deal with it. You instead just pass the problem on to the VP of Sales, who doesn't appreciate it (some feel that, "an action passed is an action completed," but that is rarely true).

A better way would be to engage George directly, in order to determine whether he can develop and execute a strategy to support the business from a marketing perspective, or whether it is really the time to swap him out.

An effective leader needs to take some time to study the background. What was the reason behind the strategy decisions? You may find out that George invested his time to build a plan a year or two ago, found that it got no traction, or his vision died on the vine. At that point, the company moved on, and George became a person just sitting there taking up space, energy and time, generating little value.

It would be amazing to see what would happen if, as a senior leader, you took the opportunity and gave George a chance to step up, and see if he could try again to perform and execute his strategy. If he can and does, he will be committed to, and engaged in, the organization, and he will be a powerful force for good. Who knows where he could take you?

TEN TAKEAWAYS

☆ ☆

1. Bad things happen to good teams. A true measure of greatness is how teams handle bad things.

2. Beware of what we, in the Army call "GOGI's," AKA "General Officer Great Ideas." Once you say, "I was just thinking," you better accept that you just increased the churn in the organization and that your people may sacrifice a necessary task in order to accomplish what they think will please the boss.

3. There are rarely any extra people hanging around these days. If someone is truly taking up space, it is an energy sponge to the organization. A leader's duty is to get these people in a position where they can contribute or move them to a position where they can contribute. (I know, I know, easier said than done, but it *must* be done.) Otherwise, you have just informed the team that you'll accept substandard performance.

4. When you are new to a leadership position, you will sometimes be presented a new opportunity to fix something within the first 30 days. Don't be in such a hurry, unless it involves safety, ethics, or the law. There's most likely a reason that your predecessor didn't make the fix. You might not agree with the reason, but there's no need to rush into something.

5. Keep communicating. When you are getting tired of hearing something, you are probably halfway there to getting the message across. There will *always* be someone who doesn't get the word. Your duty as a leader is to ensure these "someones" are kept to a minimum.

6. Leadership is a *personal* connection. You have to put your heart into it.

7. You *manage* task orientation. You *lead* people.

8. The organizational wiring diagram is like a map, but it doesn't offer anything valuable until you use it to explore the faces in those spaces.

9. A true leadership test is tough. (If it were easy, someone below you would have accepted the challenge and taken credit for it already.) I have found the toughest tests are often avoided. When you become aware of a shortfall in a performer, address it head on. Great leaders don't let these problems linger and fester.

10. When you don't know what else to do, just being there, and your team knowing that you are there, will help you do the right thing. I believe that Lieutenant at Walter Reed wanted to see if I was comfortable scratching his nose before he'd be comfortable talking to me.

2ND EXPECTATION
Manage Relationships

"No man is an island."
- John Donne

Fort Riley, Kansas—1994

In 1994, I had been in command of the 701st Main Support Battalion at Fort Riley for over a year. We had a number of challenges, and thankfully, successes under our belt. Throughout the year, however, I had one nagging challenge I hadn't overcome. I was about to discover it was more than just *my* challenge.

One of the critical things in every organization is the whole notion of managing relationships, both within and outside the company, unit, or organization.

As a leader, your people will expect you to help them manage internal relationships. Simply stated, they expect you to have a good relationship with the Human Resources department. They want you to be connected and have a positive relationship with the Vice President of Sales, and with the head of Marketing. They want you to be the type of a leader who not only talks to the Chief Financial Officer 15 days before the fiscal year ends, but is constantly in communication.

As the Commanding Officer of a Main Support Battalion, I oversaw the following responsibilities:

> 1. Providing backup support to the Forward Support Battalions (those closest to the front)

> 2. Supporting those units, like the Division Headquarters and other separate units, who did not have a Forward Support Battalion.

The Forwards were also commanded by Lieutenant Colonels, who were career logisticians. Success, for both of us, lay in being sensitive to require-ments and keeping a proactive mindset for support. Put another way, "Don't call us today at 4:45pm for an item that takes us eight hours to prepare and deliver and expect to see it today at 5:30pm."

After a year, I assessed my relationships with the two Forwards. We had a positive relationship with one Forward, and a less-than-positive relationship with the other. While batting .500 would easily get you into the Baseball Hall of Fame, it's not a formula for success on the battlefield. After thinking through the less-than-positive relationship with the second Forward, I chalked it up to his prickly personality; whatever we did, it seemed it was never quite good enough. I found that, from that point on, I took on a "never gonna make him happy" attitude when dealing with his unit.

We were preparing for a substantial training event, a rotation to Fort Irwin, California and the Army's National Training Center ("NTC") where this "prickly" unit would be in the lead, and we would support them. Our duty was to manage the stocks from Fort Irwin (food, water, fuel, ammunition, medical support, transportation requests, and so on), and deliver them to the right place, in the right amounts and configurations, at the right time, so that the Forward and his unit could accomplish their restocking and support missions as well.

Because of the prickly nature of our relationship, I found myself getting satisfied with *activity* instead of really focusing on achieving *success* for my Forward partner. I knew whatever we did, we'd hear back, "Yeah, but you forgot or didn't do *such-and-such*," and I got tired of it, so I let my capable subordinates smooth the daily waters, and in my own mind, I kept myself above the fray, saving my energy for the heavy lifting. I made do with en-suring we were going through the motions of support, rather than certifying that we were really supporting the Forward in the manner his unit needed.

Hindsight is 20/20, but I can clearly see now that I was just kidding myself, using my subordinates as a shield, and letting the Forward Support Battalion and the mission they had to accomplish flounder along.

This hit home to me when my deputy came into my office about six weeks before our NTC deployment. He started to mutter about phone calls he was getting from his counterparts in the Forward, their requests for support always exceedingly detailed and seemingly excessive ("If we need six items at 4pm tomorrow, ask for eight items at 6pm today"). At the end he said, "Well, Sir, you know that's just how they are. We'll just put up with it. It'll be over soon, and we can move on."

In hearing his tone and his belief that I shared his view, I saw that, in my arrogance and refusal to embed and demonstrate the Army value of selflessness, I had enabled my negative perspective to infect the leadership of the Main Support Battalion. My perspective had also diminished our reputation with the Forward unit. They didn't think they could count on us, and as a result of our sullen attitude and performance, we hadn't provided them a reason to think otherwise.

I had to fix this and quickly.

I called the Forward Commander and asked if I could see him as soon as possible. I met him face-to-face, and we talked about the reasons we weren't getting along. It was a bark-off session—candid, detailed, professional, and cathartic.

In the course of that important conversation, it turned out we both had plenty to work on, and we committed ourselves to do it. Most importantly, while he was candid, he wasn't combative. He said, "I don't want to win an argument, Vinny. I want to do my job, and I need you to help me."

The Commander shared where I had been difficult, and I shared where he had been difficult, and after an hour, we moved out to take care of what needed taking care of.

I went back to my team, and proceeded to get us rewired. I told them, "This problem is on me. I let you down. I learned something, and we have to get better and fast."

Additionally, I became more visible at preparations and interactions with the Forward, and our relationship moved from prickly and contentious to proactive and positive.

Our Communications Sergeant, wanting to help the process along, gave me a great tool that demonstrated our priority of support. Once we got to Fort Irwin and set up in our field site, we ensured our communication and data networks were set up and working. Our communications team set up one phone that only connected to the Forward's operations shop. No one using that phone had to dial a number. It just began ringing. The standard operating procedure (SOP) in our shop after that was, that phone was the first one we answered, no matter what was going on at the time. This was a simple yet effective solution, and it really worked at setting a responsive tone in our support.

Just as importantly, my fellow Commander now became an ally and a friend who respected our efforts and in future years offered positive input when my name came up in forums he attended.

Your people don't need you to be the type of leader who *needs to* win every argument. If instead, you step up and create positive internal relationships, your people will be able to take those positive relationships and move them up to ever-higher levels of excellence within the company.

★ ☆

Around this time, when I give my presentations in front of organizations, I usually am able to observe one participant who is grinning, nodding, and looking at me as if to say, "We are all over this. We already know all about relationships."

As I watch this well-dressed and somewhat smug individual, my mind continues to build the unspoken conversation we seem to be having. He says, "General Boles, listen, we are in the people business. We've got relationships nailed."

Suddenly, I allow the conversation going on in my head to come out into my presentation. I look at the group in front of me, and I say, "Do you think that your company already has relationships nailed? Let's do a quick test to check it out."

Take the following test to assist you in evaluating your team's relationships.

Internal Critical Relationship Test

List the critical internal relationships within your organization that you need to make sure are positive in order to get your work accomplished to a high standard. For example, who is the person in HR who can expedite a necessary action? Who is the go-to person in finance who can approve an expenditure expeditiously?

1. _____

2. _____

3. _____

External Critical Relationship Test

List those critical external relationships that you need to make sure are positive in order to ensure the best possible outcomes by your team. A few examples might be the Chamber of Commerce, local media, the mayor's office, or the fire department (you might have hazardous chemicals on site, for example).

1. _____

2. _____

3. _____

Grading Your Test

After you have finished the worksheet on the previous page, go back through all of your answers and grade the status of each relationship you listed, using the simple grading system that follows.

(+)   Positive relationship

(-)   Negative relationship

(?)   You can't get a handle on the relationship

Almost done. After you finish grading, put this book down and pick up your calendar device: iPhone, iPad, BlackBerry, Daytimer, or wherever you plan and track your time. Now, look back over the last six- to nine-month period. Notice the patterns that your clients fall into and think about the two tests you just completed and about your relationships with team members and clients.

My experience with over a hundred audiences has been that we spend more time with the (+) grades and less time with the (-) signs and (?) marks.

So how do we address and fix the state of these critical relationships?

When you look at your calendar, ask yourself, "Where and when am I going to routinely engage people internally and externally?"

You could even get a box and fill it with index cards or do something similar on your computer, and after each client or coworker's name and job title, fill out the following:

Client or Coworker's Name _____

Job Title _____

State of the Relationship: (+)   (-)   (?)

Where I routinely engage him/her:

_____

When I routinely engage him/her:

_____

If you put a question mark (?) or a minus sign (-) next to a critical relationship, you have now identified some work to be done. That work is *improving* communication.

When I present this concept to groups of leaders, someone will raise their hand at this point and say, "General Boles, there are just some people who are genuinely hard to deal with. They are hard to talk to. I am not able to connect with them. You don't understand what a pain it is to even be around them."

I say, "Then you have to get over it! You are the leader, and leaders get tough problems to solve. Your people expect you to help them manage that relationship, especially if it is a critical one. You have to meet that expectation for your people if you want to be a leader who can make their situation better."

How can you meet that expectation? Use your calendar as a forcing function. Work hard to make that relationship work with as little trouble as possible. Make interaction and engagements routine (especially with the difficult relationships). Plan every aspect of the interaction as optimally as you can. Here are some examples:

- Can you set up breakfast, coffee, or lunch with them?

- What will you say when you call Joe from finance? Write down an example conversation. "Hey, Joe, we've got a staff meeting next Wednesday. Can you and I meet for lunch afterwards or breakfast before? There are a couple of things I wanted to go over."

- As you get into a routine of planning your relationship with this team member, you will find that the relationship improves because that person begins to become more familiar.

- In the worst-case scenario, if you agree to disagree with Joe from finance, he will at least walk away from your meeting saying, "I can deal with General Boles, and I can get some stuff done."

- You will start to be able to deal with Joe and get more things done as well.

A crucial factor for you is how to manage critical relationships. Now that you have recognized that they are critical, you have to work to manage those relationships very, very well. Otherwise, you're going to find your people expending an awful lot of energy having to make up for the fact that you can't have a good relationship.

Positive relationships in the workspace tend to have a multiplying effect. Additionally, they diminish the stray voltage that saps the focus and energy of your teammates. Instead, you build value-added teams and generate a new set of go-to people to enlist to help you instead of making them adversaries.

Building these relationships is not easy. I have found, however, it is worth the effort.

A sad example of *mismanaging* a critical relationship was with a company I came across a few years ago (Company X). The client that Company X was trying to hook (Company Y) had some of the most cutting-edge products in its industry.

Company X's leadership thought that the right direction to go would be to take commercial off-the-shelf products and modify them for Company Y, as opposed to incurring the expense of new product development. For its own reasons, Company Y did not concur with this approach. Company Y insisted on unique solutions, developed with its unique needs in mind. Their message was "No commercial off-the-shelf solutions need apply."

Rather than accommodating the client, Company X's leadership went on a crusade, attempting to show the marketplace how mistaken Company Y was. They wrote open letters to the industry, spoke at professional forums, all in an ill-fated (and arrogant) attempt to illustrate the error of Company Y's ways. Not surprisingly, Company Y took a dim view of this course of action, and saw no reason to change their strategy.

The only prize Company X's leadership won for having this argument was stagnant growth. They missed out on countless opportunities to grow new products, penetrate new markets, and generate revenue and profit.

Additionally, Company X's sales force now had to carry the burden of this difficult relationship. On sales calls, the reputation of Company X preceded it ("You're the guys who say we're behind the times, right?").

This illustrates a sad case of mismanaging a critical relationship. How much more productive could it have been, had Company X tried to work with Company Y by investing its efforts in finding areas of agreement and opportunity instead of confrontation and rejection?

As we say at After Action Reviews: "Chew your words carefully; you may have to swallow them."

☆ ☆

From 1980 to 1981, I had an incredible opportunity to command a unit as a very young Officer, but it would be another twelve years until I would take command of another unit. I was pulled into other avenues in the Army, and was not in a command position again until June 1993.

Over the twelve years I wasn't commanding Soldiers, I was watching what Commanders did that worked well and what didn't work well. I would observe, reflect, and say to myself, "I don't know what I am going to do if I am in a similar situation, but I will certainly not do what that Colonel is doing," or "I better write that down and remember it because what the Colonel did is worth remembering."

Then in June 1993, I was assigned to take command of the 701st Main Support Battalion for 30 months. Things went remarkably well, and I can only say that my twelve years of observation helped a great deal because it reinforced the value of listening to great Soldiers.

The next 22 months were penance for having way too much fun in command, and I served it willingly, anxious for another command opportunity as a Colonel. That period involved some follow-on staff duties at Fort Riley, then a stint as a student in the Army's Senior Service College at Carlisle Barracks, Pennsylvania. While I was at Carlisle, the Officer who handled Colonels' assignments after graduation visited to discuss our next jobs upon graduation. I was advised that future command opportunities were slim, and I should prepare for some more staff work. Cheryl and I looked at the options and figured Washington D.C. was in our future since I had not had a D.C. assignment. So, we spent weekends touring northern Virginia subdivisions and factoring commute times.

In the spring of 1997, about three months before graduation, I received an email from an Officer at Fort Hood, Texas. He informed me he had been assigned to be my sponsor when I arrived at Fort Hood after graduation.

Proving the truth of the author Paul Goodman's statement, "Few great men could pass personnel," I got a pass from the selection board and was selected to command a 4,000-Soldier support brigade in the Army's 4th Infantry Division. There would be five Lieutenant Colonel Battalion Commanders reporting to me. The good news—I was again in command. The challenging news—I would not have the advantage of a twelve-year observation window to prepare for this command. As a result, I was challenged trying to figure out what "right" looked like in this new position.

After three months on the job, I was back at the National Training Center at Fort Irwin with my Two-Star Commander, Major General Scott Wallace. We had bonded somewhat when I first arrived in the post.

I hadn't served previously with General Wallace, however, he had a reputation as a great trainer. I was about to discover he was also a superb coach and counselor as well. With a lull in the training activity he looked at me and said, "You've been in command about 90 days. How's it going?"

Have you ever said something and as you saw the words leave your lips, you wanted to go running after them, catch them, and take them back? That's what I felt when I heard myself say, "I'm not sure."

In my experience, a phrase like that invited most superiors to question an Officer's confidence and capability to exercise the responsibilities of command (for example, "Vinny doesn't seem very confident," "We'll have to watch his performance," or, "Keep an eye on him").

General Wallace wasn't like most superiors. In response he simply asked, "What do you mean?"

I replied, with a great deal of trepidation, "Sir, I'm now a Brigade Commander in charge of five Battalion Commanders. I'm finding myself trying to avoid being the best Battalion Commander in the Brigade and instead focusing on being the best Brigade Commander I can be."

He replied, "Well, here's what I see as the difference. When you were a Lieutenant Colonel commanding the Battalion, the people reporting to you were normally Junior Majors, Captains, Lieutenants, and young Sergeants. With very few exceptions, you were the 'old man' in the organization. You were the most experienced person, because most of the people doing those jobs were doing them for the first time. It was the first time the Lieutenant was a Platoon Leader, the first time a Captain was commanding a company, the first time a Unit First Sergeant in a company was being the First Sergeant, the first Motor Officer, and so on."

My Senior Commander continued. "Having come up through the ranks and having so much experience, you knew what right looked like when doing those jobs. In other words, when you were a Lieutenant Colonel commanding a Battalion composed of a lot of inexperienced people, you spent a lot of your time making sure everyone had a shared understanding of what the standards were."

Pausing a moment, my Senior Commander then went on. "For example, you would tell your people, 'Here's how we go to the range,' or 'Here's how we will go to the field and deploy.' They needed you to take them through the standards. And you spent a lot of your time making sure that the standards were well defined, understood, disseminated through the organization, and constantly reinforced."

He then made the distinction between my former people and my current people. "Now you've moved up, you're a Brigade Commander, and you've got all of these Lieutenant Colonel Battalion Commanders reporting to you. They are just like you were. They're experienced, they're knowledgeable, and they know what to do. You're going to find that the way to relate to them is not to worry about standards because they know what they are."

"So how do I lead differently?" I asked.

He responded, "What you have to focus on now is personalities and relationships. Specifically, how you can assist each Lieutenant Colonel to do the best they can do. You will spend a lot of your time clarifying relationships—specifically, how you can assist the units and Commanders they support. If you have to teach a Battalion Commander, a Lieutenant Colonel with 18 years of experience, about standards, then we have may have picked the wrong Lieutenant Colonel."

General Wallace concluded, "I'm not saying that the Lieutenant Colonels in your charge have to know everything, but if they need to know something and they don't know it at this point, they should have enough self-discipline and energy to go learn what they need to know."

☆ ☆

When you are managing relationships as a leader, there are multiple ways to interact with your people. In my case, it turned out that there was one approach I needed to take when managing younger, inexperienced people, and a different, more detached approach for more experienced teammates.

When dealing with junior staff, relationships should be based on standards. Walk them through those standards and help them to learn and follow those standards. The goal is for the entire team to have a shared understanding of the standards.

When you find yourself as a leader in charge of people who are a lot more senior, you should assume (unless they prove differently) that they already know the standard.

TEN TAKEAWAYS

☆ ☆

1. If a professional relationship is stressing you, your folks know and act the way they see you acting.

2. Approach and engage the stressor. Be professional, be factual, and start where you can both agree on something and make it better.

3. You have to take responsibility when the relationship goes off the tracks, for your folks' well-being. That means owning up to what sent the relationship off the rails and getting it back on track.

4. The team expects you to master relationship management, and it's empowering when you do. When they know they can go to the boss and the boss will help, they try harder. If they believe you can't/won't help, they stop trying.

5. To effect change in senior, experienced team members, focus on the relationship they have with you, others, and the organization (i.e., "How can you help me/us fix this?").

6. To effect change in junior, inexperienced team members, focus on standards that tasks/processes have to be accomplished to (i.e., "This is what *right* looks like…This is what it doesn't look like.").

7. Give the benefit of the doubt in relationship management. Critique behavior, not people. The behavior is substandard, not the person.

8. Nobody (and I mean nobody) *wins* an argument. Don't have them.

9. Instead of "I'm right, therefore, you're wrong," I recommend the "Here's what I believe we are trying to do and here's what I'm seeing/hearing. What am I missing?" approach. It puts the other party in your seat.

10. Find *something* (no matter how small it seems) to agree on and build on that.

3RD EXPECTATION
Balance Risk

"People who don't take risks generally make about two big mistakes a year. People who do take risks generally make about two big mistakes a year."

- Peter Drucker

Logistics Base Anaconda, Balad, Iraq, July 2003-February 2004

I assumed command of the Soldiers, civilians, and contractors of the Army's Third Corps Support Command in July 2003. The Command had more than 16,000 people, stretching from Kuwait to multiple bases throughout Iraq, and our mission was to support more than 150,000 Soldiers who had conducted the Operation Iraqi Freedom invasion in the spring of that year.

Getting every form of supply and logistics support to 150,000 people from a standing start is a challenge in itself. My staff computed that on an average day, we had over 2,000 trucks on the roads in Iraq. (For the sake of comparison, the Wal-Mart Corporation has something like 3,000 trucks on the road every day across the entire United States.) Our trucks usually traveled in convoys of between ten and 50, depending on the mission requirement.

Our situation in the region quickly moved from challenging to hazardous because our fuel trucks, ammunition, and other supplies were out on the highways, exposed to an enemy committed to attacking them. An emerging insurgency was engaged in serious in-fighting as well as fighting us. As a result, our chief mission was to get this support out while mitigating the risk to our troops. Unfortunately, as always, the enemy got a vote in the process. We took the following careful steps to mitigate our risks.

Command Involvement: Every Commander, at every level of the chain, had to be a *Safety Officer*. Commanders didn't delegate safety. It had to be a program with the stamp of a leader's personal involvement on it.

Equipping: We had to ensure we mitigated risk through proper equipping of Soldiers and units for the tasks they had to accomplish and for the threats they faced. This was one area where we faced a significant learning curve.

There had been no briefings on Improvised Explosive Devices (IEDs) prior to our initial deployment in Iraq, but we were quickly learning about these deadly weapons from the school of hard knocks. Our initial attempts to equip vehicles by strapping additional plating onto them were dubbed "hillbilly armor" because of their rag-tag appearance. Regardless of looks, we used what we had, and we adapted to the enemy as it came at us.

The Power of Routinization: I worked for a Commanding General who opined, "Great units do routine things routinely." As a result, we put tactics, techniques, and procedures in place to deal with threats every single day. Soldiers learned and embedded certain routines in their daily actions (for example, always wearing a helmet and body armor outside the wire, always wearing a seat belt, and always loading the frequencies and call signs for a medical evacuation).

The Power of Ownership: As part of my post, I was able to command and give orders to more than 2,000 vehicles on the road every day. However, I did not want to control each one. Sergeants and Lieutenants had to own their piece of the operation and care for it. Therefore, every convoy received a convoy briefing by the team leading it before they rolled out. Every completed convoy conducted an After Action Review (AAR), citing what went well, what had to be improved, and why "it" didn't work, whatever "it" might have been. Those hundreds of young and experienced leadership teams became the hot hands of safety and security on the cold steel of Army vehicles and equipment.

Ours was not a 100 to 0 victory. Seven Soldiers were killed due to enemy action on that deployment, four Soldiers were killed in attacks on convoys, and three more Soldiers were killed due to enemy mortar attacks and helicopter crashes. We lost ten other Soldiers to non-hostile actions (accidents and medical conditions). It was terribly painful to lose each one of those brave Soldiers, and I still carry their names with me. They gave their lives for us, and I will never forget them.

At its essence, the Army must be fully capable within the following two core competencies:

> 1. The Army must capably train and grow leaders.
>
> 2. The Army needs to be able to go anywhere the nation needs it to be, when it needs to be there, with what it needs to fight and win.

One complicating factor to that mission set (among many) is that the Army doesn't get to perform these core competencies in security and safety. Wars and conflicts by their very nature are dangerous, and the job is filled with risk.

You can never truly avoid risk unless you want to put yourself in a rubber room, pad yourself, put every possible lock on the door, and have yourself fed through a small hole in the wall (assuming you trust the cook).

Risk is by its very nature inherent in everything we do. In order to move forward with a mission in the Army, we frequently exposed ourselves to the possibility of injury, danger, and everything else that goes along with that, including rigorous training demands.

Similarly, if you want to progress in the business sector, or if you want to grow your business, you have to take risks. These risks might involve the pursuit of certain contracts, making a new kind of hires, developing other lines of business, committing to research and development options, and the list goes on.

The bottom line is, you can't be in business in the United States of America in the 21st century and avoid risk. You also can't be in the United States military today, defending this nation against all the enemies we have, and avoid risk. Ultimately, it falls to the leaders to identify, balance, and take steps to mitigate risk to their operations.

As I go around the country and talk to audiences, many of the groups I talk to find themselves and their employees still reeling from the financial challenges of the Great Recession that began in 2007. Some of them are still truly paralyzed at the thought of moving out and doing new things or taking new risks. One of the reasons I believe that they are apprehensive of taking new risks is that they can't understand what caused the problems the last time.

When the most recent financial crisis hit, it hit the areas that nearly everyone assumed were "sure things." We assumed the housing market was going to continue to grow, the Internet was going to continue to boom, and the tech sector would grow with no limits. There was not enough attention paid to the mitigation of risk, and the entire country has suffered as a result.

In order to meet expectations their teams have of them, leaders must use their experience and judgment to identify and mitigate risk.

The Risk Cube

In the military, we have something we call the Risk Cube (see following page spread), which rates two critical axes of risk on a scale of one to five. The x-axis represents the probability that something bad will happen. The y-axis identifies what the consequence will be if something bad happens.

A minimal risk is represented by 1:1. There's a very low probability something will happen, but if something does happen, it's not likely to be very damaging. We'll be able to easily withstand that risk.

The worst risk is represented by 5:5. We can just about guarantee this bad thing is going to hit us, and based on how we are structured right now, we're not going to be able to handle it. Therefore, the damage received by this risk is going to be significant.

All risks don't lend themselves very easily into being categorized by ones and fives. They are somewhere in the middle. It will be a matter of discussing each risk with your people in order to understand all probabilities and consequences.

It helps to talk each risk out with your team since one person's five might be someone else's three. A financial manager looking at the risk might look at the situation only in terms of financial services, whereas, your public affairs officer or media relations professional might look at it and say, "Well, that story could look really bad in the news—that could really hurt us."

RISK ANALYSIS

Level	Likelihood	Probability of Occurrence
1	Not likely	~10%
2	Low likelihood	~30%
3	Likely	~50%
4	Highly Likely	~70%
5	Near Certainty	~90%

	1	2	3	4	5
1	L	M	H	H	H
2	L	M	M	H	H
3	L	L	M	M	H
4	L	L	L	M	M
5	L	L	L	L	M

Level	Technical Performance
1	Minimal or no consequence to technical performance.
2	Minor reduction in technical performance or supportability, can be tolerated with little or no impact on program.
3	Moderate reduction in technical performance or supportability with limited impact on program objectives.
4	Significant degradation in technical performance or major shortfall in supportability; may jeopardize program success.
5	Severe degradation in technical performance, cannot meet KPP; will jeopardize program success.

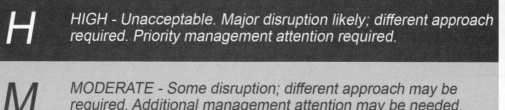

H	*HIGH - Unacceptable. Major disruption likely; different approach required. Priority management attention required.*
M	*MODERATE - Some disruption; different approach may be required. Additional management attention may be needed.*
L	*LOW - Minimum impact; minimum oversight needed to ensure risk remains low.*

Schedule	Cost
Minimal or no impact.	*Minimal or no impact.*
Able to meet key dates.	*Budget increase or unit production cost increases. (< 1% of Budget)*
Minor schedule slip. Able to meet key milestones with no schedule float.	*Budget increase or unit production cost increases. (< 5% of Budget)*
Program critical path affected.	*Budget increase or unit production cost increases. (< 10% of Budget)*
Cannot meet key program milestones.	*Exceeds APBAA Threshold. (> 10% of Budget)*

When identifying risk, it is important to identify risk as a construct of consequence and possibility (how often it will happen). Once you've identified the risk and assigned a value to it, you need to take the next step. You need to identify for your team what steps you can take to mitigate or decrease this risk. Those steps will involve both analyzing the probability that the risk will occur, and what you can do to mitigate the consequences if the risk does happen. As a leader, the goal is to reach a situation where your Risk Cube assessment is at an even-keeled 3:3.

Regardless of the best preparations, sometimes the worst will still happen. At that point, you need to work to survive that risk. One inspiring General Officer once told me, "First identify the risk. Then mitigate the risk and make sure to take steps that minimize both the probability and consequence of the risk. Then, if and when the worst *still* hits you, you have taken enough steps that you will still be able to survive and get through it." In other words, do not gamble with your team's future, and prepare for the worst case. Then, your survival will be likely.

It is vitally important to make sure your people understand the difference between a risk and a gamble. A gamble is when you go to a poker or black-jack table and put all of your chips down, betting everything. If you win, you'll win big, but if you lose, you're going to lose big and you will not be able to recover. That is not the kind of risk you should take with the lives and well-being of your team members.

★ ☆

When I was a Battalion Commander, I still remember a situation when we were trying to upload a vehicle on a system that wasn't designed to have a vehicle uploaded on it. Nevertheless, time was tight, the pressure was on, and this was our best solution.

We were planning to use a new type of vehicle that we had never used before, and we thought we had everything figured out. I thought we were in great shape. We had a Corporal ready to drive the truck and a Senior Technician to stand by if needed, and we had our other team members.

As I went around the room to each person, I noticed how each one had a different view of risk. The technical expert wanted to talk about what would happen to the hydraulic systems if we tried to lift this vehicle out and it gave way. He was thinking about the technical side of things: "Well, this hose might break. This seal might bust. But that's okay, because I've got replacements, so we'll be fine."

At the same time, my environmental expert looked at us standing there in the desert and said, "We have an environmental problem because the water table is at such-and-such a level, and the consequences could be severe because fuel could leak into the water table."

The driver had a completely different view of risk: "That vehicle is so big! I may not be able to see out the rearview mirror in the cab, so I'm going to have to put a rearview mirror on the outside that I can use."

In the Army, whenever we had an event out in a new training area or field, we would first develop a plan. Then, before we executed that plan, everybody involved came together, and we identified and talked through the details of what we were about to do. As a leader, I went around every individual, looked them in the eye, and asked, "What risks do you see?"

All of the risks that my team members brought up were equally valid, but I wouldn't have gotten the full expertise and knowledge of my team members if I hadn't given each person a chance. Every team member identified the risk as they saw it, and that was invaluable to me, especially in a new and unknown situation.

☆ ☆

When I give speeches on the topic of risk, I often think of the old Holiday Inn motto: "The best surprise is no surprise." Think of how many things would be better in our country, in our organizations, and in our lives if we always carefully looked at risk before diving in.

The expectation your people have of their leader is that he or she will have thought through all the risks. They trust their leader will help them think through the risk, and work with them on steps to mitigate that risk.

A good tool for leaders in dealing with risk is the realization that it's not just *your* risk. Risk belongs to all the entities you and your organization touch: clients, supporters, and providers. Because they are all affected, it's worthwhile, if time allows, to bring them into the risk-solution process. Don't try to face the problem alone.

TEN TAKEAWAYS

☆ ☆

1. Know whether you are taking a risk or a gamble (you can recover from taking a failed risk, but not a failed gamble).

2. Identifying and mitigating risk is a constant process. (Trust me on this. The enemy and the marketplace think up new ones all the time. You better be thinking, too.)

3. Leader behavior is believable. Your folks will watch what you say about risk, safety, and mitigation. They will believe what they see you *do* about each of those things.

4. Before conducting an operation with a high level of risk, pre-brief everyone on your team. Make sure you have a shared understanding of the risk the team faces.

5. You can't conduct successful combat operations (or corporate operations) in a risk-free environment.

6. Stay calm under pressure. Your team knows when you are facing risk, and the last thing they need is a boss wringing his or her hands.

7. There is *no* substitute for walking the ground you operate on. You will always learn something. Whenever I lost a Soldier, I walked the ground where it happened. New lessons always revealed themselves and assisted my unit in avoiding future losses.

8. Balancing risk means making choices, deciding. If you don't like the options you have, keep looking. I have found an answer is usually out there and the more senior and experienced you are, the more your subordinates expect you to find it.

9. Know when you have to truly decide. Staffs and subordinates will sometimes rush a decision. Don't be in a hurry to rush to failure.

10. Teams take their cues from their leaders. If you wonder why an organization is excitable, harried, or confused, go look in the executive suite. Chances are good that someone is displaying that behavior.

4TH EXPECTATION
Make Decisions

*"Leaders have to be comfortable making decisions
with about 60% of the information available."*

- General Colin Powell (Retired)

As the quote on the previous page reveals, leaders have to be comfortable making decisions with less than perfect information, especially in fast-moving operations, whether military or civilian. Otherwise, you will not get sufficient information in time to do anything useful with it.

An example from my career is that during Army combat operations, a Commander will have his or her forces in one location, and they will be told to go out and take on the enemy. If, at that point, the Commander says, "I'm not going to deploy my force until I know exactly where the enemy is and where they are headed," that Commander will find the enemy. Unfortunately, by that point, the enemy may already be surrounding their unit.

As a leader, you have to be comfortable making a decision with information that is often less than perfect (with emphasis on the word *comfortable*). You can't wring your hands over these decisions and say, "If only I knew more." Truly successful leaders are comfortable in their own skin when they have to decide because they have accepted the reality of less-than-perfect information.

At this point in my presentations, the more analytical members of my audiences come to the conclusion that all they need to do is build an axis with a scale from zero to 100 percent, draw a line at 60-percent, and make a decision when the assimilated information hits that line. However, reality is a bit more complicated than this linear approach. The 60 percent that one leader uses to arrive at a decision could be very different than the 60 percent criterion that someone else uses to make his or her decision.

The information we require to make decisions evolves based on our experiences, our personalities, our ideas, how we like to do things, and how we like to approach situations and problems. Therefore, in order to get comfortable making decisions while equipped with imperfect information, leaders have to know when they will, as one of my old bosses said, "decide to decide."

In order to aid Army Commanders in this effort, our doctrine has a term, Commander's Critical Information Requirements (CCIRs). These are established by the Commander and disseminated to the units in orders. They inform the units of critical information a Commander needs to know.

Some examples follow.

Inform the Commander when:

- A unit loses a Commander (either killed or wounded in action)

- A unit's equipment readiness rating for a critical system (helicopters, tanks, artillery pieces, wreckers, fuel tankers) falls below 90%

- The enemy is observed at or beyond a critical piece of terrain (If the enemy gets to hill 709, advise)

Some civilian business examples could be:

- Inform the CEO if any one of these five accounts suffers a setback.

- Inform the CFO prior to engaging in negotiations that could impact revenue/loss of $_____

- Inform the COO of any loss of manufacturing capacity lasting longer than _____ hours.

Knowing the leader's CCIRs enables the team to align their information focus with the leadership's. It also ensures that the critical information leaders need to make decisions gets to them in time to allow them to positively impact their environment.

The 4th key expectation subordinates have of leaders that President Clinton revealed in 2001, is that leaders will make decisions. One of the key things leaders have to understand is that their people expect them to make decisions.

That statement usually flies out across my lips and lands in the audience with a resounding thud. And in the world of professional speaking, thuds do not ensure repeat business.

Put another way, my audience is having an internal monologue: "Okay, we brought a retired General to speak to us here at the XYZ conference, and one of the supposedly 'critical' things he tells us is that leaders make decisions? Boy, oh boy, is he a smart one. I'll bet he got an A in his leadership class! Everyone knows that leaders make decisions!"

Yes, of course, leaders are decision-makers. Leaders are paid to make decisions, especially the demanding ones. My purpose in making this point is that leaders lose sight of the fact that they are responsible for all the decisions an organization makes, not just the ones they individually make. Let me share a story that made this clear to me.

A Great Job

In July 1993, I was living and working at Fort Riley in Kansas; I was a Commander in the 701st Main Support Battalion. More specifically, I was assigned to the Support Battalion in the First Infantry Division, which at the time had over 18,000 Soldiers. When any of those 18,000 Soldiers ate, drank, fueled, shot, drove, broke something, needed medical attention, or had to have it shipped some place, one of the 900 Soldiers entrusted to me was going to touch one of those 18,000 Soldiers. Simply stated, at 17 years in the Army, I was in my dream job, both as a Commander and as a logistician.

There I was, a New York City native, transplanted to the Flint Hills of Kansas. I had been on the job for about 30 days, and I was walking down to one of my warehouse operations, when I passed a guard shack. Walking into the guard shack, I met a great young Soldier. Let's call him Private First Class or PFC Smith.

Smith was one of those people you find in an organization, who, regardless of their rank, experience, background, or pedigree, had made up their mind to do a great job. Smith was going to own his piece of the organization and be the best at his job that he could be.

You have all seen people like this in organizations. It can be somebody on the loading dock who runs the loading dock and it's "their" loading dock. Or the receptionist who is "that" receptionist and makes everything happen. Or that great person in a hotel who makes sure that the rooms that she cleans on her floor are going to be the best rooms in that hotel, and she is going to consider you a fortunate person because you get to sleep in one of her rooms.

They just want to be that way because they are part of the organization. These are the people who don't just hang out. They show up and they step up to make the difference.

PFC Smith was one of those people. I spoke with him for a few minutes, and then I asked him what he did. He told me that he was a gate guard.

I asked him, "What does a gate guard do?"

Smith replied succinctly that he had two basic responsibilities. First, he checked all the vehicles coming in to make sure that we had all of the information that we needed, and that they were coming from the type of organizations that we supported. Smith was also able to direct those who were in the incorrect locations to the right areas.

Smith's second responsibility was to check the vehicles that were departing to ensure that what they had on the manifest was what they had on the vehicle. Let's say they came in to get two radios, four tires, and one weapon. Smith's job was to check the manifest and make sure that they didn't drive out instead with 104 radios, 104 weapons, and 102 tires.

As I talked to Smith, I watched him go through a couple of vehicles. Within a few minutes, it was apparent that he needed no help at all from me to get his job done. He owned his piece of the organization, making it possible for me to walk away, content with the fact that I had that piece of the organization covered for that day. Smith was, as we say in the Army, "all over it."

All Over It

I left Smith and proceeded down to the operations shop. I knew what it would be like when I (the new "boss") walked through the front door. Everyone would jump up, come to attention, and the place would flood with a general sense of nervousness. Written on my people's faces was, "What's the boss here for? Did we do something wrong?" Today it might be, "Get off your Facebook page!"

In order to both limit the startling effect of my arrival and to enable me to quietly observe the operations team, I entered via the back door.

The room was about 30 feet by 30 feet, and this was the place where decisions were made about who could accomplish different support tasks.

They were working at a humming pace. Requests were coming in, people were being met, things were getting processed, work was being accomplished, effectively and efficiently. I had for the second time that day found a part of my team that was "all over it."

Idiosyncrasies and Pet Peeves

Let me digress for a second. Have you had a boss who has had a pet peeve? What about a boss who has some kind of idiosyncrasy—something that is not illegal, unethical, immoral, unsafe, or fattening, but is kind of strange and different?

As a leader, one of my idiosyncrasies is that I couldn't stand a phone to ring more than three times. I don't know where that quirk came from, but at about two and a half rings, and I would start looking around the room, seeing who would get to that phone.

I was a proud leader that day in 1993, watching my people work efficiently, like talented players on a skilled soccer team, knowing each others' moves.

I was standing next to a desk in the operations shop, when the phone began ringing. Everyone was engaged, there was no one available to answer the phone, and with my need to answer telephones before they hit the third ring, I reached over, picked up the receiver, saying, "701st Main Support Battalion, Support Operations Section, this is Colonel Boles. How can I help you?"

There was a brief pause on the other end of the line, and when the voice began to speak, all I heard was a weak, "Uhhhh…" The person on the other end of the line was clearly nervous. They had not intended to get Colonel Boles on the phone.

"He probably wanted to get Private Jones or Corporal Jennings," I thought. This wasn't an uncommon occurrence.

I said to the caller, "Look, I know you're nervous and probably didn't expect to get Colonel Boles. This is the Support Operation Section. If there is something you need, just tell me what it is and I'll hook you right up with the person or the section that can take care of what you need."

Again I heard…. "Ooh."

Let's try one more time — "Look, I know I'm the last person you expected to talk to and I'm probably not the person you wanted to talk to. If you'll just tell me what you need, we'll get you hooked up with the right section."

After a pause I heard, "Sir, this is Private First Class Smith at the front gate. I'm supposed to call the operation shop whenever Colonel Boles shows up."

After I got over my shock, I replied "Really? Just stand by."

About that time, one of my Sergeants at the front of the office began to look around, and spied me in the back of the room. Surprised to see his Commander there, he jumped up immediately and said, "Colonel Boles!"

"I have a message for you, Sergeant." I said.

"Yes, Sir!" he said.

"PFC Smith at the front gate wants you to know that Colonel Boles is here."

Who Decides?

As funny as that story is, both to remember and tell on stage, when I sat down and thought about the day's events that night, I realized that it wasn't humorous at all. The United States Army had made a decision that I was qualified to support, train, deploy, and take care of those Soldiers and their families. But someone had made a decision that my people had to be warned when I was out running around because I couldn't be trusted to meet anybody unannounced. Who made the decision that the organization had to be protected from me?

I never found out who made that decision, but the point that I make and pass on to you is that a lot of decisions will be made in your organizations. So who decides to decide in your organization? In order to truly step up and be a leader in your organization, you are expected to make decisions.

As a leader, even though you don't make every decision, your organization believes that you would be comfortable with the decisions that are made. Your team also believes that you have approved every decision made. If you are not comfortable with a decision because you didn't know about it, at least your people will believe that you are comfortable with the people making those decisions.

How often do you ask about decisions in staff meetings? Decisions are the lifeblood of an organization, when they are made in a timely, effective, coherent fashion. They move the organization forward, they inspire confidence between the leader and the led, and they reinforce positive action. Folks get in the habit of passing critical information accurately and moving out to execute decisions correctly.

To become adept at making decisions, you have to do three critical decision-making tasks:

1. Accept there is no perfect information. You'll have to go with what you have when it's time.

2. Ensure you have thought through how you "decide to decide." What are your CCIRs?

3. Disseminate the CCIRs and revisit them on a routine basis.

TEN TAKEAWAYS

☆ ☆

1. There is no perfect information to make decisions. You make decisions based on a combination of knowledge and bringing your experience to bear on sifting through that knowledge to get to a decision.

2. As you make decisions, get in the habit of asking yourself, "What is the reason I'm making this decision?" You may be doing someone else's job at the expense of your own, and they are not getting the benefit of the decision-making experience.

3. Establish and disseminate your CCIRs, so you and the team share a common view. They will get clarity on how you "decide to decide" by getting an understanding of the information you need.

4. When you have asked every question you can think of and poured over the information for the upteenth time and you have to decide and are still not sure, then trust your instincts. Ask yourself, "Which option am I most comfortable with?" and go with that. Then if it doesn't work out, you'll at least not kick yourself for ignoring your instincts and find yourself saying, "I knew I should have...."

5. Whether it's a mentor, coach, friend, or counselor relationship, get in the habit of talking about decisions you have made or will have to make. There will usually be a nuance or a perspective you missed.

6. When drilling out a tough decision, think of five leaders you admired and reflect on what questions they would be asking and ask those questions.

7. When going around the conference table or the list of teleconference participants, specifically ask each one the following: "What am I missing?" and "What do you recommend?" Get the participants to step up and engage, so it's their process even though it's your decision.

8. Whenever possible, explain your decisions by stating what is being decided and what caused that decision to occur. This explanation gives the team a window on your decision-making process. Also, if there is a timeline factor to the decision (e.g., "For the next 60 days, no credit card use over $200"), ensure that factor gets disseminated as well and gets reviewed at the appropriate time. I still remember at the end of the fiscal year we would put restrictions on requisitions for 30 days so we could close out the fiscal year. Four months later, I met a clerk who asked, "Are we ever going to be able to reorder, Sir?" You have to follow up.

9. When leaders change, so will the CCIRs. Their "60%" will be a new equation to solve and you need to know, so you can make decisions. As a new leader, get in the habit of discussing the CCIRs as part of your transition. If you get a new leader, make asking this question part of your inbrief.

10. Just as every batter doesn't hit 1000 and every sales call doesn't result in a signed order, every decision may not work as you expected. Revisit the decisions, see what you missed, learn from that review, and move on.

THREE QUESTIONS
for Leaders to Ask and Answer

*"If they can get you asking the wrong questions,
they don't have to worry about answers."*

- Thomas Pynchon

I n my Army service, I had the opportunity to do things that most people would never be able to experience. I was stationed around the world in various units with different jobs and responsibilities. I also was never assigned in the same place twice.

This variety and the energy it brought gave me the chance to do amazing things with remarkable individuals.

It's made me positive that if or when I get to heaven, the heavenly version of a finance or personnel clerk will inform me that I owe back half of my retired pay because I obviously had way too much fun in the Army. I will pay that willingly.

Every coin has two sides, however, and on the flip side of mine are some long days. I would pray for somebody to take those days from me, if anyone would.

There was the phone call on Super Bowl Sunday, when the 49ers were defeating the San Diego Chargers: "Fire in the training area, Sir. Tent destroyed, three Soldiers missing, everything in the tent burned down. We are going through the area now to search for the missing Soldiers."

A call on Operation Iraqi Freedom in 2003: "Sir, we just had an attack." We had been receiving mortar attacks daily. Usually, only one or two shells hit isolated areas of the base due to the enemy's poor aiming skills and equipment. The attacks were more harassment than anything else.

"Sir, this wasn't a mortar attack. This was a rocket attack. Seven rockets went off over the dining facility at dinnertime. Going through the rubble now. Looking at multiple wounded."

I still remember the cold feeling that pierced me and twisted my stomach in knots when these and other calls came on my watch as a Commanding Officer.

I'm not to be pitied. If you are going to lead this nation's treasure, then responsibility for what happens or doesn't happen falls at the feet of the Commanding Officer. A former Chief of Staff of our Army, General Gordon Sullivan, once said, "You can wring your hands or you can roll up your sleeves, but you can't do both."

So, after these tragic events, I would circle back and try to figure out what went wrong. After all, we hadn't planned for events to unfold this way.

What I found in *every* occasion was that there was always someone during the review, who would let me know that "I knew that (tragic event) was going to happen."

"Well, if **you** knew it was going to happen, why didn't **you** say something?" was my response.

The answer I received would always be something like, "Well, you knew what you wanted, Sir, and I figured you knew something I didn't."

I was very surprised to find out that people were quickly willing to suspend their own good judgment when they believed that they would have no ability to affect change. At that point, I realized that it was incumbent upon me to set a climate where people were free to say, "Hey, wait a minute! I don't think that's going to work."

This suspension of good judgment is not an occurrence unique to the military either. Take the story of the NASA engineer, Robert Boisjoly. Boisjoly was a booster rocket engineer for Morton Thiokol, the company that manufactured the space shuttle's rocket boosters. In the winter of 1986, NASA was preparing to launch the space shuttle Challenger. The temperatures in Florida were unseasonably cold. Boisjoly weighed in and informed his leaders that if launched in cold conditions, the shuttle would be "a catastrophe of the highest order," and the leaders agreed to recommend a launch delay to NASA. NASA's reaction was not a welcoming one: "My God, Thiokol—When do you want me to launch—next April?" was the reported reaction of one shuttle program manager.

According to Boisjoly, the Thiokol leadership team met this reaction by putting on their "management hats" and reversed their no-launch recommendation.

The Challenger exploded within minutes after the launch, and the investigating commission concluded that the cause of the explosion was the reaction of the booster rocket "O" rings to the cold temperatures.

When I was a Major, I worked for Steve Marshman, a Battalion Commander in Desert Shield/Desert Storm. Our personalities were very dissimilar, but he trained and respected me and we made a difference in supporting a great unit at a challenging time. Imagine being a Soldier in Europe in 1990. The Berlin Wall has fallen, the Soviets are leaving Afghanistan in failure, democracy is breaking out in Eastern Europe, and we get informed in November 1990 to take a Europe-centric force, deploy it to Southwest Asia and eject the Iraqi forces from Kuwait.

That wasn't in our battle plan. One of the reasons I believe we successfully accomplished this mission was because of two questions Steve would always ask: "What's the system?" and "Who is in charge?" A few years later and over my own time and experiences, I added a new #1 question: "What's the standard?" I added this third question when I had to work a number of integrating actions on a strict timeline in 1992, when we had to deactivate our Brigade in Germany to support the drawdown of the Army from over 780,000 Soldiers to 485,000. All the equipment had to be brought to standard and turned in, transported to its new owners, and taken off our books. With many sets of different eyes looking at what we were doing, I found if I didn't get clarity and agreement on the standard we wanted to attain first, then no system or delegation would help.

The lesson I want to share is that EVERY time I or a unit I was in failed to accomplish a mission or a shortfall occurred or a critical event turned tragic, it was ALWAYS because I didn't ask and answer these three questions:

1. What's the standard?

2. What's the system to attain the standard?

3. Who's in charge of the pieces of the system?

Remember, I said ask *and* answer.

There are a lot of people who are really good at asking questions and never bother to run the answers down. You have to ask the questions, and then you've got to verify, validate, and confirm the answer.

1ST QUESTION
What's the Standard?

"Hold yourself responsible to a higher standard than anybody else expects of you."

- Henry Ward Beecher

It happens so often that I get surprised if it doesn't happen. You get called up to headquarters for a teleconference. Whatever the venue, you get tapped to execute something new. It could be a new mission, a new job, a new task to accomplish, or perhaps a new client to take care of.

As the meeting concludes, your impulse is to jump into the car, have a conference call with your team from the interstate on the way home, all to make the point that "We need to get going on this!"

I have a recommendation…. Wait!

Before you drive away, before you call your team together to launch them off, sit on your car keys. Sit on your car keys, think through the task you just received, and see if you can answer the question, "What's the standard?"

If you come up empty as you roll this question around in your headspace, get out of the car and go back inside headquarters. Don't come out until you have the answer or before you and your boss have agreed that the first part of the task is to establish and confirm the standard.

If you can't explain the standard to yourself and your team, you have no right to be frustrated and upset when your team doesn't attain that standard.

If you do define the standard for yourself and your team, then, as one of my Chaplains used to say, you will all be "singing from the same hymnal." When you have a shared understanding, people won't be spinning their wheels trying to figure out what you want. They will expend their energy getting after the standard you have defined.

Clipboard Corporals

You have to do more than just talk about and articulate what the standard is. You also have to make sure that the standard is attainable.

It wasn't uncommon when I first came into the service to see martinets or what we used to call "clipboard corporals" in the Army. They knew what the standard was and were very, very good at assessing people's performance against the standard. They would say something like, "You met the standard. You met the standard. You, you, and you didn't meet the standard. You three who didn't meet the standard fail—hit the road."

The cut-and-dry standards these clipboard corporals supported was the way the Army used to be run. We were simply supposed to bring people in, identify those who met the standard and keep them, and throw out those who didn't meet the standard. This method comes across like a sink-or-swim approach, which is not the process you would expect to see in learning, values-based organizations.

The Army recently came to grips with this approach in the years after Operation Iraqi Freedom, when our expectation of a quick win shifted to an extended conflict. It was challenging meeting our enlistment numbers in order to field the force to fight this war. I was in the training base, receiving new recruits and conducting the training they needed to operate in the specialty they had signed up for.

Even then, with our enlistment challenges, we still had Drill Sergeants whose success in their job lay in kicking trainees out of the Army. They would tell me, "My job, Sir, is to identify what the standard is and if these kids can't meet the standard, it's my job to throw them out of the Army."

That view was shortsighted and it required some attitude adjustment for our Drill Sergeants. They needed to learn how to get their trainees to meet the standards without compromising those standards.

Changing the View

At one point, I remember talking to a bunch of Drill Sergeants who were saying, "We need to get these kids out. They can't meet the standard."

I said, "Well, let me tell you how I see it. I'm looking at the fact that every year 170,000 young men and women are joining the United States Army. All I need to know about the young men and women that we are training is that they have volunteered to come serve their nation in a time of war."

I thought I had their attention now. "When the heat is high, the pressure is on, and the bullets are flying, these young men and women have volunteered to come from their homes wherever they were and join the United States Army knowing that during their time of deployment, they are likely going to combat. I think they've already met the toughest standard, and that's the standard of choosing to dedicate themselves to this country."

I spoke to the Drill Sergeants about their mission, as I saw it. "What we are going to do now is insist on and maintain our high standards. But we are also going to take on as one of our missions ensuring that we assist our Soldiers in getting to those standards." They understood what I was saying, and they did a great job of implementing this new mission in the following months and years.

You Have to Get Comfortable with the Color Gray

I have observed a number of leaders who were not very successful (it happens). They sit behind their desks and are compelled to paint everything in black and white. For example, they say something like, "Everyone who met the standard is great, and all of you who didn't meet the standard, it's terrible to have you in my organization, and I can't wait to throw you out."

If one of your people has a moral failure, that's one thing. But if the standard is technical or physical and the person has demonstrated dedication to the work and the standard, then it's the job of the leader to assist that person in getting to that goal.

Great leaders insist on high standards and never back off of them. If the leader's people aren't meeting the standard, the leader should look in the mirror as a first step toward the change needed for the team's success.

Articulate the Standard

The standards can be taught, approached, and reached in a variety of ways. Standards can also be based on many different factors, including time, resources, and money. Whatever standard you use, you should put metrics back into the standard. For example, you will say, "If we do this right, it's going to look like the following." How will you accomplish your goal?

At some point, we had a new Lieutenant who had just shown up in the unit. He reported in to his direct superior, and his superior looked at him and said, "Lieutenant, you're going to be a Platoon Leader of the First Platoon. You have about 60 Soldiers. The First Platoon didn't shoot very well at last month's firing range. I want you to make sure they do better."

That was it; those were all the instructions the new Lieutenant received. He went back to his team after the meeting, sat down, looked at them, and asked, "Okay, so how do we do better?" The Lieutenant used the exact same terms that his superior had used. Both of them set the team up for failure by using a vague, innocuous standard.

Instead, imagine that the standard had been refined from the get-go. What if we told the Lieutenant two very specific standards?

1. All 60 individuals are going to qualify.

2. Everybody who fired at the last range is going to fire at least one level better than they did before. So if they fired at the marksman level, they are going to fire at the sharpshooter level next time. If they fired at the sharpshooter level, they're going to fire at the expert level next time. If they fired at the expert level, we want them to maintain their expert-level marksmanship.

These standards are crystal clear. There is no possibility of misunderstanding, and the Lieutenant can start working with his people right away to achieve the specific standards. As opposed to "Do better than you did last time," the refined and specific standard allows the Lieutenant to succeed.

Always seek opportunities to articulate, clarify, and reinforce the standard you want your people to accomplish tasks to. You will find you have to do this often. People change, their previous organization may not have had a standard for the task, or that organization may have had a different standard entirely.

Another reason for this repetition is that people will listen to what a leader says, but they will believe what they see that leader do. For example, if I state that physical fitness is a priority, they hear me. However, if I look like the last time I ran was when I heard the doughnut shop was closing or the Stop-and-Shop was running out of cigarettes, they won't believe me. My behavior isn't congruent with the standard. If you say something is a priority and then don't train for it, resource it, or spend time on it, your people won't see you "walking your talk."

One of the first great Officers who trained me was Major Edward Hart at Fort Knox, Kentucky, from 1977-1979 during the post-Vietnam era. Ed was the Executive Officer (second in Command) of the 544th Maintenance Battalion. Ed joined the Army in 1959 from ROTC, and with the Vietnam build-up of the 1960's, he went from the rank of 2nd Lieutenant to Major in six years! It took me eleven years to make the same progression. Because of the post-Vietnam drawdown, Ed retired as a Major 14 years later. During this time as well, Officers went through multiple "Reductions in Force" ("RIFs") So Ed had accomplished a great deal by just being allowed to stay in the Army. While he could have been a Colonel at any time, the force structure didn't allow for it. I'm sure he desired to serve at higher levels, but he never complained and the benefit for our unit was that we had a really experienced 2nd in Command who knew what "right" looked like, kept us from spinning our wheels, and focused us on the "right" things, both individually and collectively. He was so steady and dependable, we used to say, "If he ever gets nervous, you'll know it's time to get nervous."

Ed looked out for young Officers like me. He'd drop by your area, see you in the headquarters building and simply and effortlessly contribute to your development with a question, an insight, or a task: "Read this article and tell me what you think."

One day, I was trying to get something done and it wasn't going well. Ed inquired about the reasons (I was in charge—this was about standards and systems) and discovered I had told someone to do the task and now at the eleventh hour, things had gone poorly and I was attempting to pull everything together. I can still feel the hard edge in his voice when he informed me, "You are an Officer. Never tell someone to do something if you won't enforce it. You'll show them you don't care about your profession and you are not serious about holding them to standards, which means you don't care about them." Although that conversation took place more than 30 years ago, I am transported back in a flash and can feel the gravity in his voice and the serious look in his eyes as he was sizing me up to see if I was getting it.

I never forgot that moment, and every time I put orders out from then on, I would look around the room, sensing who was getting it and who would be my next leadership concern.

TEN TAKEAWAYS

☆ ☆

1. Ensure you know what the organization standard is. You may have to dig, but the people who care are usually happy someone is asking about the standard, and they'll provide it.

2. Understand that standards evolve over time. Learn who the standard-keeper is in the organization and what their review process is.

3. Unless you are the subject matter expert on the standard being attained, avoid the effort to invent a new standard. The standard was put in place for a reason. As we said in the Army, "If 90% of the Soldiers could meet 90% of the Army Standard 90% of the time, we'd be doing pretty well."

4. It is OK to set stretch goals and reward individuals if they exceed the standard. Be careful about taking punitive actions against those who meet the standard but not your stretch goal. If you punish those people, you have shifted the focus from the organization's standard to your stretch goal. The mixed signals you send may not be worth the pain.

5. Backbrief standards. A technique we have in the Army is the Commander's backbrief. You receive a mission and are given a period of time, depending on the situation, and then in person or digitally, each subordinate "backbriefs" the senior leader by stating how they understand the assignment or mission, asking questions for clarification, and synchronizing the mission timeline. This backbriefing really serves to highlight points that need clarification ("When I said morning, I meant tomorrow morning") and to identify gaps ("I want you to deliver to X not later than 2 pm, but X won't be there to receive the delivery until 8 pm").

6. If you don't enforce a stated standard, then whatever is convenient for each individual will become the standard. So if you have 100 teammates, you have 100 variations on the standard.

7. When you enforce a standard or correct something that is not performed to standard, remember to correct the behavior of the individual rather than attack or abuse the individual for not meeting the standard. For example, it is correct to say, "You need to redo this report. The format is detailed on the I drive. Have it to me by COB tomorrow. Let me know today if you have a problem accessing the I drive." It is unhelpful to say, "You are a real genius. Now I have to waste our time getting you to re-do this. What other screw-ups are you making that I haven't found yet?" Based on 40 years of leadership experiences, I can promise one thing: Leaders who use the unhelpful technique will have employees who will eventually forget what task you criticized them about. They will never forget how you treated them. You will have to expend a large amount of your leadership capital to overcome your unhelpful choice.

8. If you find that the organization is being challenged to accomplish a certain standard, you are probably not alone. If it is a critical, time-sensitive task such as safety, then as a leader you have to focus, or the organization will get frustrated at failure and may try non-standard work-arounds. These work-arounds may be short-term fixes that eventually exacerbate the problem the standard was designed to address. You may need to get the subject matter experts in and execute what is called a "deep dive," where you, your team, and the experts really delve into the issue. For example, I found that we had a personnel shortfall in a few of my units two levels below me. As a result, we did not have certified, school-trained Soldiers in these few units. When I saw the aggregate numbers, this shortfall was masked. Only when we went unit by unit did we see the impact of this shortage. My trained Soldiers were pulled to other staff sections, and the section doing the real work lacked sufficient staff. This "deep dive" view enabled me to redirect resources to the right locations.

9. If it's an important standard, routinely focus on it and reinforce it. For example, every quarter, units brief their Commander, two levels up, with

their training status for the quarter just passed and their plans for the next two quarters. These briefings become a critical part of the training routine and ensure we commit the resources early enough to conduct the training required. I had a Commanding General who said that he thought great units were units that did "routine things routinely" and did them well.

10. Before you address a performance shortfall over a standard, especially if it is multiple levels below your level, check to ensure the standard was communicated clearly through all those levels. The standard may have been sidetracked or misunderstood (see Takeaway #5 on Backbriefs).

2ND QUESTION
What's the System?

*"Everything must be made as simple
as possible, but not simpler."*

- Albert Einstein

My wife, Cheryl, is a football fan (AKA fanatic). She has a great appreciation for and understanding of the game. Wherever the Army put us, she always found a team to cheer for (as long as they weren't playing her beloved Buffalo Bills). In her honor, let me make the following segue.

Once you have articulated the standard, the next step is to ask and answer the following question: "Do we have a system in place that will ensure our people can accomplish this standard?" Imagine a football coach whose standard was "Win." However, if the coach fails to build a playbook for the multiple situations of the game (offense, defense, special teams, etc.), any success they enjoyed would be by accident. In fact, since they didn't know how to execute, they would be standing around and in football, if you don't keep your feet moving and your head on a swivel, that is the fastest way to get blindsided.

Nothing is more frustrating to a unit than throwing them a standard without ensuring they have a system to attain the standard.

Once you have a standard articulated, then you have the responsibility to focus your team on accomplishment of the standard. You teach them how to put a viable system in place and then to use that system to get to the standard.

So the critical question is, "How do you find the right system?" What is the system by which you are going to achieve your desired outcome? Here are a few roads you might have to travel down to put that system in place.

1. You may find out that you don't have a system, so you better go develop one (it's a new team that has never played together before).

2. You may find out that you have a system, but it's been a while since you used it and everybody doesn't know it (it's a transition period, for you, the team, the industry, and you have to refocus).

3. You may have a really old system that could be dusted off and made to work now. Remember when Coach Darrell Royal of the University of Texas brought the full house backfield of the 30's back and modified it to the Wishbone Offense?

Whatever road you take, it needs to lead you to a system that you can install, that everybody understands, and that everybody can utilize in order to accomplish the standard.

The System in Marksmanship Training

Going back to the Lieutenant and the marksmanship lesson from last chapter, let's think about what system he can utilize to attain the desired standard.

The Lieutenant is responsible for the training, readiness, safety, deployment and if deployed, utilization of about 60 Soldiers. His standards are:

• All 60 Soldiers pass to the minimum standard of marksman if they haven't fired before with the unit.

• If they have fired with the unit at the last range, they are to increase their proficiency by at least one level (i.e., from marksman to sharpshooter or from sharpshooter to expert).

• If a Soldier fired expert at the last range, they must attain the expert standard again.

The Lieutenant now has a standard, and he now needs a system to achieve his goal. He sets up a Marksmanship Training System. He identifies the standard for each individual Soldier, based on each Soldier's current abilities. He answers the following questions about each Soldier.

1. Where is that Soldier today in terms of his or her abilities? Shooting a weapon is a learned motor skill, and the more each Soldier does it, the better he or she gets at it.

2. How much time do we have before the next range? Do we put them on a firing simulator? Or would they achieve better on the firing range?

3. Which Soldiers are really in trouble (AKA "weak swimmers") and are at risk of not meeting the standard? What additional training time and type of training do they need? Where and who are the shooting subject matter experts who over their career have excelled at training new shooters? (Drill Sergeants in Basic training for example, routinely have to take newly inducted trainees from around the country and train them in Basic Rifle marksmanship in nine weeks.) Can you integrate these experts into your training plan for the shooters for whom shooting is difficult?

In building a system, you often have to find one that works across the spectrum of employees. If special training or qualifications (certain education level or certain physical attributes, e.g., so tall, type so many words/minute, etc.) are needed (especially for newly integrated/procured systems for example), you need to verify that you can acquire personnel with those skills and you must clarify who conducts the training. (Is it part of the fielding contract or do you have to pay extra?)

To return to the central idea, if you give the team a standard, you have the responsibility to ensure they are in possession of a system they can utilize to attain the standard and that they understand how to use it.

2003-2004: When It Didn't Work

In summer 2002, we were preparing to ship additional equipment to Kuwait to support the forces that were going to be deployed to conduct the initial invasion of Iraq, known as Operation Iraqi Freedom. The plan was that we would begin off-loading equipment from our floating warehouses known as "Pre-Po" ships, which stands for the term "Pre-Positioned." The equipment was configured in unit sets and we would array it so that upon their plane landing in Kuwait, a unit could move to the equipment site, draw the equipment, and begin training for the invasion.

Due to the "Peace Dividend" of the 1990's that was caused by the implosion of the Soviet Union and their Warsaw Pact allies, the nation chose to send the Department of Defense on a procurement holiday, putting off purchasing equipment that was required. With no near peer competitor to the US military, such spending could be delayed, and the government assumed we would always have enough time to purchase when we needed to. The suddenness and effects of the 9-11 attacks quickly proved that assumption wrong.

One of the challenges in this system and its assumptions, however, was that the dormant manufacturing and funding resources, unexercised for almost ten years, can go hot right away and do it fast enough and with enough capacity to produce everything required.

The Army staff calculated that the risk assumed with this system was to the tune of over $56 billion (yes, with a "b") of equipment and supply shortages.

What this situation specifically meant to me was that the equipment sets I was storing and maintaining weren't stocked with 100% of the required assets. For example, one of the critical shortages for our logistics units was in materiel handling equipment, known by the acronym MHE. MHE consisted of forklifts and container handlers, which enabled units to stock large amounts of supplies and move them around the storage areas and, when required, to pick up and move the storage area to a new location on the battlefield. It was required for all types of supplies, and every supply and storage activity needed them. One of the critical types of MHE was an item known as a Rough Terrain Container Handler (RTCH, pronounced "wretch").

We were short a large number of RTCHs in our sets. They were expensive, and we didn't really need a large number of them until we went to combat. Once we had to go to combat, we had to get them, and the Army went to a company in Sweden that made a high-quality RTCH and bought all we needed. They were bought, however, just prior to the invasion of Iraq in March 2003. They became, in what is known in the fielding process, as a "drive-by fielding." Units had no time to train on the equipment but were told the equivalent of, "Here are the keys. There is Iraq. Move out."

Initially, things worked all right, however, our readiness ratings began to slip. Since these RTCHs were new pieces of equipment, we did not have any subject matter experts to diagnose and repair the systems. We were also challenged to identify what to order since we had not loaded their parts lists into the DOD supply databases. Finally, our Soldiers had not trained on this equipment, so they were doing their best but learning as they were driving, which is not recommended.

We didn't know what we didn't know and consequently, there was a great deal (in fact, way too much) of discovery learning occurring.

We were able to get the company in Sweden to send a technical representative to Iraq and for the better part of two to three months, he traveled on our convoys throughout Iraq to every site we had one of his company's RTCHs operating. He trained operators and maintenance personnel, used his satellite telephone to order parts we needed, and took the time to show us what "right" looked like in the RTCH world.

Before he departed, the corporate heads wanted to visit Iraq and tour the fielding sites. I remember walking through the yard with the CEO and one of his RTCHs was carrying a loaded 20-foot container across the yard very high off the ground at a unique angle and the CEO commented, "I didn't know it could do that."

We relearned the lesson that when you substitute speed for diligence and attention to detail, you pay in the long run. We spent untold hours and dollars trying to keep the fleet maintained so that our supply support operations stayed on track, all because we didn't have the funding up front to field and train our folks on these systems. As a great Soldier once told me, we got in a hurry and it was a "rush to failure."

Summer 1990—Spring 1991: When It Did Work

When the Army develops equipment to meet a requirement, one of the key documents is the fielding schedule, which states who gets how many, in what configuration, and when. The fielding has to be synchronized with the unit getting the equipment. If you show up to Fort Campbell, Kentucky in December to issue helicopters to Fort Campbell units that are deployed to

1965, Confirmation Day with Mom and Dad.

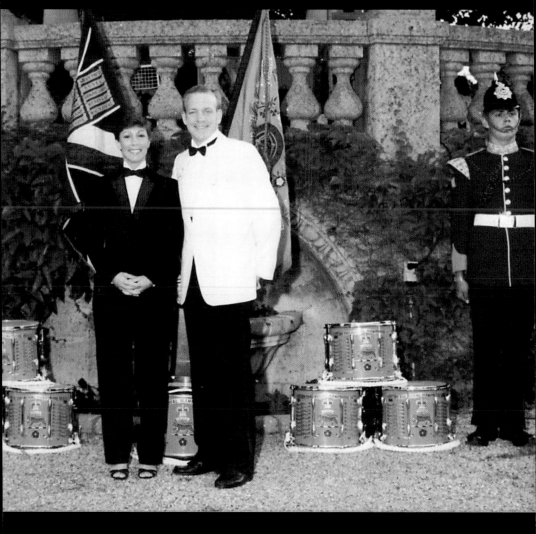

June 1986, With the British in Berlin
to celebrate the Queen's Birthday Ball.

May 1991, Redeployment home.
Cheryl met every bus until I came home.

June 1993, Getting ready to take command of the 701st
Main Support Battalion with Major General Mitchell
looking on—the best job I ever had.

Sept 2004, Aberdeen Proving Ground, Maryland.
Another 701st reunion—for over 20 years now,

May 1997, Army War College, Carlisle, Pennsylvania.
An annual tradition, the Laundry Room Ball, dress was
"half formal" (note Cheryl's jeans and my shorts).

February 2004, Back home in Germany after
Operation Iraqi Freedom 1. Who knew at the time there
would be eight more years until Operation New Dawn.

May 2004, Mom and Cheryl at Yankee Stadium.
They are waiting on the "pitcher."

May 2004, Throwing out the first pitch at Yankee Stadium.
I can still hear Bob Sheppard announcing "Ladies and
gentlemen, welcome a NY City native home!"

September 2004, Aberdeen Proving Ground, Maryland. Accepting
the colors as the Army's 33rd Chief of Ordnance from the 26th Chief
of Ordnance and my mentor, General John Coburn.

July 2009, (L-R) my brothers, Kevin and Kiernan, Mom and I
at Fort Meyer just before the retirement ceremony.
("We're not missing this!")

July 2009, Retirement Ceremony at the Pentagon,
LTG Metz, Cheryl and I. Where do we go from here?

January 2011, Louisville, Kentucky—with 600 of my new friends. *People Get Paid to Do This?*

Afghanistan, you are going to have a long wait.

Also critical in the fielding process is the disposition of the equipment the unit swaps out. Put another way, "If I get a new one, what do I do with the old one?"

In the summer of 1990, I was in the 2nd Armored Division in Germany. We had been identified to receive the newest upgrade to the M1 tank, called the M1A1 Heavy. As I was briefing our Commanding General on the swap-out plan, he asked me what our system and standard was for swapping out tanks with parts missing on them. Not having conducted a swap-out of this size (over 120 tanks), I stumbled a bit. He clarified things when he told me, "No tank needing more that $1,000 in parts will be swapped out." When you consider, at that time, that M1 tanks cost in excess of $2 million, that was setting the bar pretty high. Units worked at it all summer, operators and maintenance crews climbing over their old systems, tightening, replacing, testing, all to turn them in. Imagine if you had to do that to a car you were trading in at the dealership!

Whenever the Commanding General toured the motor pools and met with leaders, he would always ask, "What are the average $/tank parts you are turning in?" He stayed on that question and never let up. Finally, in the fall of 1990, we said goodbye to the last old M1 at the railyard as it went off to its new home in a warehouse in the Netherlands and began to get familiar with our new M1A1 Heavies.

The Rest of the Story

In August of 1990, Saddam Hussein's Army invaded and occupied the country of Kuwait. Over the fall, the war planners determined that a larger force was needed to eject Saddam Hussein's Army from Kuwait. Since the Berlin Wall had fallen in 1989, the decision was made to take forces in Germany and the U.S. that had been programmed against a Soviet and Warsaw Pact threat and deploy them to Saudi Arabia to remove Saddam Hussein's Army from Kuwait. This became known as Operation Desert Shield / Desert Storm.

In November of 1990, we received our deployment orders. We would load our equipment on ships at the port of Bremerhaven, fly to Saudi Arabia, link up with our equipment, and head to an assembly area in the desert to conduct our Pre-Combat Checks and Inspections (PCCs and PCIs) and be ready to conduct combat operations. During the pre-deployment process, we were informed that the 2nd Armored Division (Forward) would be attached to the First Infantry Division (The Big Red One) from Fort Riley, Kansas.

The M1A1 Heavy fielding schedule was spaced out over multiple years and the First Infantry Division was to get their tanks later in the 1990's. They arrived in Saudi Arabia with early versions of the basic M1 tank. The Army leadership, therefore, made a decision to give the 1st Division newer tanks, and the tanks they gave them were the ones we had turned in. Furthermore, our Commanding General was designated to be the Assistant Division Commander for Support for supply, transportation, maintenance, and medical support.

Imagine if we hadn't cared the previous summer about turning in the best tanks we could. Our battle buddies in the Big Red One would have suffered with substandard equipment and our Commanding General would have inherited substandard systems that he failed to maintain.

We had a standard, and we had a system, and those two things came together when we needed them to.

TEN TAKEAWAYS

☆ ☆

1. The key to execution of a system is usually not in the individual steps or components of the system but at the intersecting points where the system breaks down, the places where transfers, transitions, or handoffs occur. If a system does not execute, check the places where there is an intersection of functions and/or people.

2. It's as important to ensure the system is not misunderstood as it is to ensure it is understood. If anything can go wrong, it will. You cannot assume that just because you understand it, someone else's conception isn't 180 degrees removed from yours.

3. The first time Soldiers in basic training assemble and learn to march as a unit, it is tough to watch and painful to be part of. But if the Soldiers stay with it, they get better. Don't throw out the system because of initial hiccups.

4. "You got to know when to hold 'em, know when to fold 'em": As the Kenny Rogers' song "The Gambler" states, you have to make choices on when to stay with the system you have or when to start over. The leadership challenge is having the experience and professional judgment to know when it's time to throw out your system and start over. There is no equation or school solution for this. I have found, over time, that a few criteria help me to decide it's time to throw the system out:

> • If it's not getting better, you bring all the affected parties in, commit to fixing the system, climb all over it, and it's still not getting better.

- If the contractor is not living up to commitments and the system is not performing to promised capabilities. Some contractors "bid to win" a contract vs. "bid to perform" the contract. Check with your legal team to ensure you can execute the termination clause.

- When you have another readily available substitute system.

- If you keep discovering more problems than solutions as you get more experience.

5. When we bought our present home, my wife, Cheryl, found the house, negotiated, and bought it in three days. I was on a trip and saw the house the day before the closing. She called me the first day and told me, "It feels like home." Then she asked for my advice. Of all the things I told her, she told me one suggestion really resonated with her: "Walk through the house five-six times over the next three days. If you find yourself liking it more and more each time, that's a positive indicator. If you find more and more things wrong with it, that's probably a negative indicator." She found herself liking it more and more, and it has served us well so far.

6. Smoke out "Dr. No." Change affects people. When change occurs, everyone wonders, "How will this impact ME?" Most people take the concept of being on a team and being a good teammate selflessly and want to help the team succeed. Some, however, can't get past their sense of "I don't like it." If left unchecked, these naysayers can stall or, even worse, derail the system. When you have initial and follow-on briefings in preparation of fielding the new system, pay attention to the verbal and non-verbal cues you observe. They will tip you off to individuals who may be less than supportive. Also, watch out for those who fight the change by hanging onto the old processes with their own workarounds. This situation causes confusion as some say, "Oh, I have the option to change or not?"

7. Go Slow Early to Go Fast Later: Production cycles don't go from producing at the initial rate to full-rate production in the blink of an eye. You have to plan for the ramp-up. It is the same when you put a new system in place. For example, if you need to produce 120 widgets in twelve months, you probably don't start at ten per month for twelve months. More likely,

you produce three the first month, followed by ever increasing production rates until you hit the 120 mark.

8. Have your team prepared for success beyond your greatest expectations. It may work better, way better, than you thought. Then everyone else wants to get in on the action. As the accurate quote states, "Victory has a thousand fathers, but defeat is an orphan." When it goes great, get your team that made it go great out in front. Rewards, accolades, articles, photos in the company magazine/newsletter/website all reinforce that they are on a winning team.

9. Focus on the investment payout the system will bring vs. its cost: "Gang, if we install this, we'll be faster, cheaper, more effective, and more efficient." There are people who know the price of everything and the value of nothing. Their focus tends to be cost and expenses instead of value. If left unchecked, these people can stall needed improvements.

10. Have In-Process Reviews: The 100 people that were present when the new system came on line are probably somewhere else a year or two down the line. After the initial flush of excitement that comes with a new fielding fades, it is easy to lose focus. Schedule, at a minimum, 3-, 6-, 9-, and 12-month reviews to ensure the focus stays on and embeds the system in the organization.

3ᴿᴰ QUESTION
Who's in Charge?

"Remember Rule 14, Vinny: When in charge, be in charge."

- Major General (Retired) John Mitchell
U.S. Commander, Berlin (1984-1988)

Have you attended a staff meeting where a difficult and quite possibly contentious issue is being reviewed? As the meeting winds down to its conclusion, do you look around at the folks filing out and find yourself wondering, "Which one of these folks is going to fix this?"

I have yet to find the CEO whose lament is, "I don't have enough meetings to go to," despite the fact that meetings harness the collective energy to maximize the productivity of the group. Put another way, meetings are supposed to enhance the work experience!

Are your meetings focused? Are the attendees there to address and resolve critical issues and move ahead? Or are meetings just a collection of people who appear to be spectating and appreciating the issues, observing rather than engaging?

In the Pentagon (and I'm sure other places) we called that a BOGGSATT (Bunch of Guys and Girls Sitting Around the Table Talking). Translation: a group not expending their energy toward accomplishing anything.

This group might appreciate that there is a problem, but they've got their hands in their pockets, when what is really needed is a group who will engage the problem, roll up their sleeves, and resolve it.

To preclude BOGGSATT, allow me to discuss with you what I see as the critical factor in BOGGSATT eradication: Leaders must identify the individuals responsible for execution and resolution of the issue and then give them the requisite authority and latitude to do so.

Transforming a BOGGSATT into Something Viable

Now that you have your team and they are attending meetings and "appreciating the problem," how do you transform them? After all, in many cases they have been rewarded for "appreciating the problem" and this behavior may have become ingrained over a long period of time.

I found two techniques that are very helpful in transforming behavior. These techniques include the agenda you establish for your meetings and how you choose to end your meetings.

An Alternative Agenda

The core purpose of a regularly scheduled meeting for a work group is to transmit and clarify the information the work group needs in order to bring their value-added efforts to the enterprise. To be truly value-added, the meeting has to transmit and clarify this necessary information up, down, and across the team. Specifically, managers and leaders can't do all the talking, and the teammates on the line and in support roles can't sit mute and just nod their heads.

To get your people engaged, you have to change the normal agenda. What normally occurs is that the support staff (personnel/HR, marketing, finance, etc.) start the session with their statuses and requirements. What this normally means is that the line team goes last at the end of the meeting. Usually by then, the line team has been on the receiving end of the staff's task list: "I need all the performance appraisals by COB Friday" (probably said on a Thursday); "Get your budget estimates in for next year by next week's meeting" (usually while you are trying to execute a year-end close of this year's budget and getting the last big order out); "Every employee needs the opportunity to select their healthcare plan by _____" (they just got it today and the scuttlebutt is that they can't really pick a plan until the state you are in decides if they'll form a health care exchange or not).

Bottom line, by the time the line team has filled up their notebooks with the staff's requirements, their desire to hang around and contribute to the cause has dampened (they are probably thinking the longer they stay, the more tasks they'll receive). I remember an Officer who used to refer to our weekly

Command and Staff meetings in Germany as the weekly "Command and Stab" meeting, and he was responsible for the agenda!

So to make it value-added for the line troops, you have to shake up the agenda. Here are the steps I took:

1. The Operations Chief displayed the unit calendar for the next critical period (could be a quarter, a month, the year, — decide what works best for you). That enabled all the team, staff and support, line and operations to have a shared view of the future.

2. Knowing that the line and operations team would have to bring that calendar to fruition, I would ask what questions/comments they had. They would usually ask the five Ws (who, what, where, when, and why). It was revealing to see which staff members were ready with the information and which ones gave a bit of "Humma...humma."

3. I would then go around the table and ask each line and operations representative for a status update. At the end of each update, I would inquire what assistance that person needed from me or the staff. This reinforces that the staff exists to support the line and operations team.

4. Then and only then does the staff get to pass on information, keeping it short. Most of their requirements can go out by email or handouts. I asked they brief "by exception," meaning that they discuss only those areas that were either high performing or out of tolerance.

It took a few meetings to get in a groove. Once we found that groove, meetings were shorter, more focused, and the calendar became the key document for focusing the team.

Ending Your Meetings

At the end of a normal meeting, fatigue sets in. The most excitement you'll see is when you say, "Dismissed." Part of the group will quickly exit, wanting to get back to the safe haven of their office or work section. Another group will hang back to either see the boss about a matter they want to discuss or conduct some additional coordination with the staff.

I adjusted how I ended meetings to make them more value-added by doing two things:

> 1. Before adjourning, I would ask if there were any questions. It was rare if there were any. I would then go around the table and ask each key leader and staff representative the following question: "What are the critical things you have to do before our next session?" I must forewarn you, this is a big change for a team. They are accustomed to departing after saying in unison, "No questions." You make them uncomfortable when you ask what they have to do next. As a result, most leaders stop asking after one or two meetings. Hang in there! I have found if you continue to ask that question for three to four meetings, the team pays better attention, they share information, and they discover disconnects earlier : "You are doing that? I thought I was."

> 2. After the meeting is over, I would have my top team (in the Army, this was my direct subordinate Commanders, and only the top team—no substitutes) in my office, or I waited for the room to clear, and I would have a five-minute "what else" session. This extra session showed how much I valued this group. It also diminished frustration at the meeting; this group held their tongue in public if they were bothered by something, knowing they would have an audience with me immediately afterward to express their concern. This "what else" session also brought them closer together as a team.

I found this process helpful, and I offer it as an alternative to the meeting process you may have now. It's not perfect, but to quote the title of a recent book by General Colin Powell, *It Worked For Me.*

This process does not require a uniquely military, hierarchical, top-down model. It can be consensus-based among the people involved. The key is the word "identifying." The individuals have to know they are responsible. It's as my Battalion Commander, Steve Marshman, from Desert Shield/Desert Storm used to ask: "What's the system, and *who's in charge?*"

So, how do leaders decide who to put in charge? There are a number of options when making that decision. Let me discuss a few of those options.

By Position/Job Description

This is pretty straightforward. If you occupy a specific position in the organization, you have specific responsibilities to discharge. Two examples: If you are the dispatcher in a transportation firm, then you identify what assets go out on what routes to accomplish what missions on what time schedule. If you are the doctor, you prescribe the medications for your patients.

Panel Selection Process

Often used in the Civil Service. The applicants for positions complete an application packet that outlines their qualifications and experience. A panel of individuals, usually senior to the applicants, will then review the packets, score them, rank-order them, and identify the top three to five individuals who score the highest. The results are forwarded to the individual designated as the selecting official, who then reviews the files and either makes a selection or, if no candidate is deemed suitable, restarts the process.

A key component of the panel process is ensuring that the panel has a complete description of the responsibilities of the job and management's understanding of the qualifications needed for the job (e.g., education, previous critical assignments, etc.). The panel process usually falters when the job description is bland or when another job description is dusted off and the blanks are filled in.

Interviews

Either as a pattern of personal preference or if it is a senior position in the organization, leaders also conduct interviews. Much has been written on the interview process. In this day of lists, one can go to any employment or business information website like Google business and see comments that identify the "10 Top Interview Questions" or "10 Best Ways to Answer the Top 10 Interview Questions." The only limitation is how willing you are to plow through the web and find them.

Additionally, the setting will vary based on the job, from a conference room, an office, or on occasion, the shop floor. I have seen an interview process for instructors that required teaching a class as one component. It enabled the school to determine if the candidate had the requisite knowledge of the subject and was comfortable in front of students.

Having conducted multiple interviews in the Department of Defense and in the corporate sector, I have concluded that interviews are ultimately about the interviewer answering two questions:

> Do I feel a "connection" with this person? Will he or she fit into the group?
>
> At the conclusion, can I "see" this person doing this job I am interviewing him or her for?

That really is it. All the questions, lists, and recommended responses are oriented to get these two answers for the leader doing the choosing.

Let me share a story about two of my interview experiences.

In April 1981, I was a Captain, wrapping up my first five years in the Army life at Fort Knox, Kentucky. I had been exclusively leading Soldiers with service as a Platoon Leader, Company Executive Officer (the #2 leader in a Company), and on two occasions, a Company Commander. It had been a great apprenticeship in both leadership of people and management of the critical tasks involved in conducting maintenance operations. I was overdue for an assignment, and as I looked to the future, I saw few opportunities for troop duty with Soldiers. The future looked like a series of staff tours, possibly in nice locations, but without the daily Soldier interaction that kept my motor running.

During this thought process, I was approached by an employment firm that had established a niche linking junior military Officers like me with companies seeking junior managers and leaders. I went to a seminar, passed their screening, and put my resume in their database.

I had four initial interviews, and they were positive enough that I was asked up for second interviews by the four corporations. The interviews were straightforward office interviews, and I was scheduled for a third session. However, I want to focus on one interview that was a little different.

On a Friday afternoon, the employment firm reached out and asked if I would fly to the West Coast on Sunday for a Monday interview with a company that needed a sales representative. I agreed and headed West. My handler at the employment agency informed me they were having some challenges filling this position for the client. As I recall, I was informed I was the fifth or sixth candidate. This was critical because the employment firm was only paid when the position was filled, and they were paddling hard but hadn't accomplished it yet.

I arrived on Sunday afternoon, went to the hotel, and was contacted by an executive of the company, who informed me he was taking me to dinner. Now, being around Soldiers and the Army had built in me some sensitivity to working folks on Sundays. I didn't mind doing paperwork, but I didn't as a rule pull folks in on Sundays as a routine. There had to be a critical requirement to make that call.

I told him I didn't need to take his Sunday away and thanked him for offering his time. I would just get something from the hotel and start Sunday.

He refused that option and informed me he'd pick me up shortly. We went to a restaurant downtown and had a dinner that lasted over two hours. When I thanked him for his time, he replied, "It's part of the process."

The next morning, I was picked up for breakfast by another executive, interviewed, and then transported to the headquarters building. Once there, I was given a small office and different executives came to the office with two items in hand: my resume and a list of questions to ask. For the next nine hours with a lunch break (that was also an interview), the process unfolded. Without exception, they all had the same list of questions. After the fifth iteration of "Tell me about yourself?" it was getting difficult to maintain my concentration.

At the end of the day, I was told I had done well and that they would be in touch. I inquired about the unique process the company was using, especially for a first interview.

They explained that this process weeded out candidates who didn't possess the will or the stamina to excel at sales craft. As one executive said, "Anyone can be upbeat with a customer at 9 a.m. That's the first call of the day. We want the person who can stay upbeat and keep going at 6 p.m. when it's their last sales call and they have heard nothing but 'no' all day. Those are the folks we want, and this is how we find them."

After arriving home and getting counsel from some great Sergeants, I decided to remain on active duty. That interview process, however, really stuck with me as an example of a company that had developed a process to select a front-line sales force that everyone in the organization could believe in.

In July 2003, I had been deployed to Balad, Iraq as the Commanding General of the 3rd Corps Support Command (3rd COSCOM). It was the main logistics base for the 150,000+ members of the coalition that conducted Operation Iraqi Freedom. The 16,000 Soldiers of the COSCOM were the supply, maintenance, and transportation engine for Combined Joint Task Force 7 (CJTF-7).

As I liked to say, "If any of the 150,000 members of the coalition eat it, drink it, fuel it, order it, drive it, fly it, shoot it, talk over it, or send a message on it, the 16,000 Soldiers on this team provide it."

As the Commanding General, I was authorized an Officer to serve as an aide. The Officer would be a Lieutenant with about 2 ½—3 ½ years of service as an Officer. This aide's duty was to ensure I was kept on schedule, kept informed, and that I could reach out and connect with whom I needed to connect. The aide's ultimate purpose was to make the best use of my time, which is the most critical resource for a leader because you don't get any more of it. Twenty-four hours is all you get.

Having been an aide for almost two years, I had an appreciation for the challenges of the job and I felt I knew how to employ an aide.

Before my arrival to Balad, I had informed the team that I wanted to select an aide from within the unit rather than bring one with me. The day before I assumed command, five Lieutenants were lined up for interviews.

Because you will spend a large amount of your waking hours with the Officer you select, I found it important to really feel a "connection" with the Officer. The person didn't have to be my "buddy," however, I needed to feel comfortable with that person on long days, and especially in a combat deployment, those days were going to get longer. My key was to assess if the Officer could remain calm under pressure and be comfortable in his or her own skin.

The first Officer entered and within five minutes was so nervous, he began crying and hyperventilating. I had simply asked him, "What do you think the duty entails and how do you think you would do?"

The next Officer entered and when asked the same question replied, "It sounds like it'd be cool."

The third Officer informed me the position would look good on his record and would help his next assignment.

After completing the interviews, I selected an Officer who served the unit and me very well.

But I took the following lesson away. I had been unfair to the unit and those Officers. They and the people that sent them up for the interview didn't know me. They were flying blind and trying to accomplish an impossible task under the pressure of a combat situation by trying to support a Commander they didn't know as best they could.

In retrospect, I should have arrived, asked the Chief of Staff to select an Officer to serve for 60 days as I felt my way through and got to know the unit. Then, when I asked for candidates, there would have been greater clarity.

Wake-Up Call

As I said at the beginning of this book, over 33 years of great service to the nation and now in my civilian career, I have discovered that, whenever something goes bad, there's usually always somebody who knew it was going to go bad.

It is ultimately the leader's responsibility to create a climate where that person could step up and say, "Wait a minute!" That is the wake-up call that all leaders need. The following are the steps to take:

1. Always be able to articulate what your standards are.

2. Verify and validate that you have a system everybody understands.

3. Use your system to accomplish that standard.

4. Make sure that your people know what piece of the action, what piece of the system, and what piece of the standard they are personally responsible for.

One of the critical leadership tasks I found myself engaged in, especially as I got more senior, was to identify obstacles to progress for my units and to take their excuses away. This was brought home to me shortly after my selection to One-Star General was announced. A colleague with whom I had served asked if I would do a presentation for his unit. In his office before the presentation he expressed some of his frustration when he said, "Don't change, Vinny, once you pin on that star. The leaders I work with schedule meetings, I lay out my issues (resources, time, personnel, etc.), and they shrug their shoulders and tell me, 'You better figure that out!' I thought leaders were here to help."

That comment hit me. It reinforced that being a General Officer might change some aspects of leadership, but the team expected me to be more than just a taskmaster. I was there to assist the team's efforts and to ensure their success.

If you take excuses away, identify who is in charge of what, and reinforce their efforts, your team will move heaven and earth to make you successful, to make you look like a hero, and more importantly, to lift the organization because it is *their* organization.

Final Thought

Being in charge is demanding. For some, the demands are offset by the rewards (both intrinsic and extrinsic). Others find the responsibilities and interactions too onerous and overwhelming and will choose not to lead. A leader I knew once expressed his essence of leadership this way : "The only way to make a diamond is to take a piece of carbon and submit it to heat and pressure. Sometimes you get a diamond, and sometimes you get carbon dust."

He was focused on making diamonds.

TEN TAKEAWAYS

☆ ☆

1. When you are in charge, there are specific things you have to accomplish. It's important to also get an understanding of the implied tasks. You won't just meet the production schedule (specified), you will do it safely and ensure that leaders have the required updates (implied).

2. Focus on the position description first. Once you identify a person to fill the position, then focus on the objectives for the person. Offer that person a mix of organizational objectives (budget, revenue targets, safety inspections, for example) and professional objectives (write an article twice a year for a professional journal, be a presenter at the annual industry conference).

3. MMFI: A chaplain once told me to remember that every Soldier has two nametags. One has his or her name on it. The other is over his or her heart. The nametag over the heart contains the same four letters: MMFI for "Make Me Feel Important." How well you make those in your charge feel important will determine your success and the team's success.

4. "Who's working for whom?": As a leader, you are in charge of doing your job and making sure your subordinates are doing their jobs. If you catch yourself doing their jobs, you are not doing your job.

5. Put counseling sessions on the calendar and stick to them. Never cancel a session. If you have to move it, reschedule it. It will show how serious you take these sessions, and your folks will do the same.

6. The most important thing you can do in a counseling session is the last thing you'll do—that is to schedule the next one. When you tell someone in April, "We'll talk again in September" and you follow through, you set the tone.

7. When you take a new leadership responsibility, make these three questions part of your transition process. Ask them of superiors, the outgoing leader (if you can link up), peers, and subordinates:

- "What is going well in the organization, and how do you know that?"

- "In what areas does the organization need to improve, and how do you know that?"

- "If there was more time, what would you want to get around to?"

By asking these three questions, you will get a concise picture of areas you need to maintain (going well), need to fix (not well), and see some azimuths for future actions (things your predecessor didn't get around to).

8. When conducting routine counseling sessions, don't make them complicated. The best Officer I ever saw accomplished a counseling session in 15 minutes with three data points: 1) "Here is what you have done well." 2) "Here are some areas I'm concerned about in the last period. Let's talk about those." 3) "Here is where I need you to focus for the next period." To this day, when I run into this Officer's subordinates, they still comment on how positive this technique was.

9. What "cues" are you giving off? If you want a competent, confident, and capable organization, chances are so does your team. If they are not exhibiting these behaviors, first do a little introspection on your behavior. Are you inhibiting those behaviors with your attitude or demeanor? Teams will home in on the leader's temperament, and you may not even know you are doing certain things that are getting in the way. In 2004, shortly after I returned to the United States for a new duty, my mom was hospitalized. I was concerned. She was in good health and in her eighties, but it was my mom. For about a week at work, I was withdrawn and not very effusive. Finally, the Chief of Staff asked an Officer who had known me in another job to come see me and ask if everything was all right. When I expressed surprise about his concern, the Officer said I better snap out of it, "Because,

Sir, you are new here, and the people think they have done something wrong." The next day found me whistling in the hallway.

10. Trust your instincts: There will be times when everyone will tell you to take a certain course of action. The analysis, the financials, and the market have pulled the team, and the train is getting ready to take off. Everyone is smiling and nodding at the conference table. But you are still not sure. Trust your instincts. You are in charge for a reason. Make them drill it out again and again; tell them you are not convinced and they have to "sell it" to you. Make it hard to get to yes. Go seek out a mentor or a disinterested party and have that person review the action. After that, if you are still not convinced, don't do it. If you make the wrong choice and they were right, you can apologize and make it right in the future, but you'll be able to live with yourself. If, however, you talk yourself into the course of action against your instincts, you will kick yourself over and over again, and you will be very difficult to live with.

TWO REASONS
AND THE SOLUTION
for Stress in Teams

*"To achieve great things, two things are
needed: a plan and not quite enough time."*

- Leonard Bernstein

In my new life of speaking to corporate and association audiences on the topics of "Leadership" and "Supply Chain Optimization," I hear a number of concerns as I go around the country, interacting with audiences. No matter the audience makeup or the region of the country I find myself, two related concerns repeatedly surface:

1. The constant pace of change and the stress it brings into the workplace.

2. The difficulty of finding a work-life balance in this environment.

One factor that I see (and have experienced) that contributes to these concerns is that in this age of globalization, mobile devices, and email, we are always connected and we are, therefore, expected to always be available.

A few events illustrate how navigating this reality has been a challenge for me.

Email really took off in the military in the 1990's. I still recall my boss telling me to take some vacation (it's called leave in the Army). I went to the shore in Texas with Cheryl and left my email alone for five days. Even with an out-of-office notice, I returned to over 1,000 emails! (While that was disturbing, what is more troubling to me is that right now, after reading this, some of you are puffing out your chest saying, "1,000 emails! That's nothing. I get over _____ emails a day!")

I made an agreement with Cheryl that even on "leave," I'd check my email twice a day for no more than 30 minutes, so I'd avoid spending my first two days back at work, trying to wade through the digital onslaught.

I recall getting my first BlackBerry device in 1999 when I was a Colonel in Washington D.C. Two years later, one of our General Officers on the staff retired. He had been an Officer in the Signal Corps, the branch of our Army that handles communication and information management systems. At his farewell luncheon, he remarked that he hadn't requested a BlackBerry when they came out. He said this decision came to him one day when he was in the men's room at the headquarters, and he heard an Officer checking his email while seated on the commode. The retiring General Officer said, "There are some things that I'm just not going to do."

This constant connectedness isn't just a military phenomenon. Recently, I was speaking with a friend who is a successful school superintendent. He told me wistfully, "Just look how I come home at the end of the day and compare that to how my dad came home in the 1960's. When my dad came home, he sat down, lit up his pipe, relaxed, read the paper, watched 30 minutes of Walter Cronkite or Howard Smith on the nightly news, talked to my mother about how the day went, and ate a nice dinner. He might have asked us kids how the day was going. Then he got ready for bed and woke up the next day, ready to get back to business."

The superintendent then talked about his own homecoming each night. "I come home and I am tied to my BlackBerry, checking phone calls, getting excited and worked up, looking at email."

I share these anecdotes in order to emphasize that stress is now a constant part of our daily lives. If you find someone who says, "I want a job where I'm not going to get that kind of stress," that person will have to move somewhere I've never seen before.

Let's take a few pages for a quick overview on stress as a concept.

In his book "The Stress of Life" (1976), Hungarian endocrinologist, Hans Selye, explores a way for thinking of stress and how to deal with it. He characterizes stress as either "eustress" or "distress."

Eustress (also termed positive stress) is defined as manageable stress, "which can lead to growth and enhanced competence." Some examples of eustress are the stress on the first day of a new job or dealing with new things faster than you can process. But it's manageable; you get better, and in a while, you reflect back on those days as a necessary rite of passage to grow into the new job. Another more physical example is when one gets into a fitness regimen after a long layoff. The initial muscle pain and discomfort, if you stick with it, is soon offset by your enhanced competence. Weight you couldn't lift and distance you couldn't traverse are soon replaced by renewed energy and improved fitness.

The key is to accept the discomfort of eustress and work through it, knowing it will get better and looking forward to the payoff.

Selye characterizes the other form of stress as "distress" (also termed negative stress), which is "Uncontrollable, prolonged or overwhelming stress that is destructive."

Distress resists all your efforts; you come in earlier, stay later, take work home, enlist more support in terms of people and resources and it gets no better.

Selye discusses the effect of stress on individuals. But in my experience, I have also seen how stress can affect the organism known as the "workplace."

To deal with stress, Selye discusses the concept of adaptation. Adaptation is the "change that takes place as a result of the response to the stressor." We can view this as how you and the organization choose to deal with the stressors you come into contact with.

I recall when I was with General Wallace at Fort Hood. As we reviewed an event that had not gone to standard, General Wallace stated that "bad things" happen to "good" units. The true measure of a unit's greatness is not the avoidance of bad things, but rather how the unit handles those bad things as they occur. Does the unit encounter difficulties as eustress? Do they accept the challenges, learn from them, and see that the challenges lead to "growth and enhanced competence"? Or does the unit experience difficulties as distress, which overcomes the team and leads to reactions that are "uncontrollable, prolonged, overwhelming and destructive"?

General Wallace's point was that you and your team haven't necessarily failed when something untoward occurs. The road to greatness or failure is found in how you respond to the challenging event. How have you built the unit to adapt to stress? Stress is a given, and it's going to stay with us in our modern world. Acknowledge that stress is part of your reality and realize that we will not be judged by the fact that stressful things happen, but by our ability to handle stressful things with balance.

Bernstein's quote at the start of this chapter reflects the thought that some stress is needed to achieve greatness. Let's now look at what causes distress and how as a leader you can work at optimizing your team's performance when challenges occur, so your team can experience the manageable stress that Selye speaks of as opposed to dysfunctional distress.

THE TWO REASONS

"Stress: the storm before the calm."
\- Cameron Conaway

In 33 years of Army life, I have been a part of a number of organizations and have observed those organizations and many leaders. In those 33 years, I have heard all kinds of reasons for stress.

Based on my experience, let me offer a simple, accurate observation on the subject of stress, specifically as it relates to "distress."

Distress flourishes when an organization (and the people in it) are not operating in accordance with the organization's stated values, norms, and behaviors. The organization is not "walking its talk." And the organization knows it is not performing the way it should.

Sometimes the problem is a small thing that affects a portion of the workplace. Other times, the problem is something larger with more impact across the force.

Another constant I have observed in stressful situations is what I call "Casablanca Leadership" or the "I'm shocked" leader (a la Claude Rains as Captain Renault in the movie "Casablanca": "I'm shocked, shocked there is gambling going on in this establishment," Captain Renault says as he is handed chips from the croupier).

I have been part of (more than I'd like) situations where a leader has performed in a substandard manner and was then removed from the leadership position. There were any number of reasons for the removal and excuses given for the behavior: incompetence, moral turpitude, leadership toxicity (the list is limitless). While the senior leaders expressed surprise at the substandard behavior, the subordinates expressed surprise that we were surprised at all. They might have said, "We could see the problem. How did you miss it?"

Hence, the challenge. How do leaders establish an organization that "walks its talk," and when the walking gets off track and generates stress, how do you know, so you can fix it and get back on track?

The Notion of the Center Line

In 1982, I was in Berlin, Germany. The Berlin Wall was still up and divided the citizens of Berlin into eastern and western sectors. Berlin was an enclosed and divided city with our French and British allies and a few million German citizens for company, surrounded on all sides by the Soviet Union Army and the forces of the Warsaw Pact.

My initial assignment was as an Organizational Effectiveness Officer (OE), a fairly new Army program. Basically, I served as an internal Organizational Development Consultant for the Commanders and Staff. As with most new programs, it was met with a variety of responses, which ranged from, "I'm already short on people and you are using them on THIS?" to "I'll use it if I have to" to "Hmmm, tell me more. This program might help me."

Thankfully for me, my immediate boss had been trained as an OE and I had a supportive Commanding General and, therefore, a supportive command climate.

One of the events OEs facilitated was a transition seminar. The incoming Commander would meet with the team (subordinate Commanders and the staff) they had inherited. The transition seminar was designed to minimize the stress and waiting time for the organization to assimilate the new Commander. It also gave the incoming Commander the opportunity to think through his or her approach to command and how to disseminate that approach to the team. The day-long session gave the participants the opportunity to sort out who was on the team, get to know them, identify any near-term issues that needed to be addressed, and enable the leader to highlight "Here's what's important to me."

There were three Infantry Battalions in the command. The Commander of one of them was Lieutenant Colonel Jouni Keravouri. LTC Kervouri reached out to me and asked if I'd assist him with a transition session. It was the first of multiple engagements with that unit over the next year, and I

THE CENTER LINE

COMMANDER

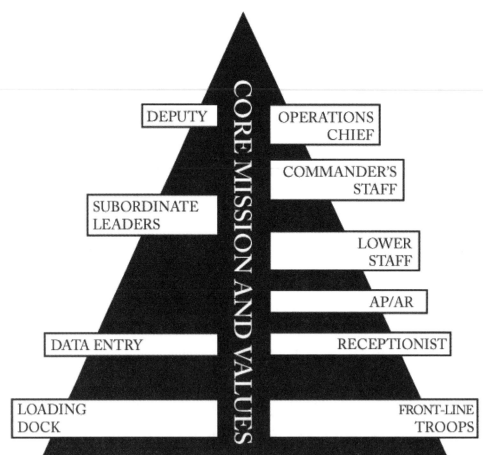

DEPUTY

OPERATIONS CHIEF

COMMANDER'S STAFF

SUBORDINATE LEADERS

LOWER STAFF

AP/AR

DATA ENTRY

RECEPTIONIST

LOADING DOCK

FRONT-LINE TROOPS

CORE MISSION AND VALUES

learned a great deal about leadership on the front lines, where I saw up front what works (and what doesn't).

At the session, LTC Keravouri took a great deal of time to explain to his senior leaders in the battalion the importance of aligning the unit at every level around the core mission and values. He drew a triangle and then drew a line down the middle. *(See triangle diagram on preceding page.)*

He then spoke to the group and here is my recollection of how he expressed his thoughts:

> "This is the 'center line.' It starts with me at the top of the organization. As we move down the organization, the people at lower levels move further away from the center line. When you get to the bottom, the ones who have to execute are the furthest removed from what the mission and values are. So our duty as leaders," and he looked at each leader in the room, "is to ensure that folks at each level get as close to the center line as they can. The closer their alignment, the less confusion, and the less dysfunction, the greater synergy of our efforts. When we are out checking, this is one of the things to check for. How aligned is everyone to the 'center line'? Do they know what the center line is and how they impact it?"

For the next two years, I watched that Battalion Commander superbly command his organization, and wherever you saw his folks, they were aligned on the mission and core values. As importantly, this Commander ensured that his "Center Line" was synchronized with his boss. That was key because the great idea didn't belong just to him but was a vehicle to bring success to his team and to his superior's team as well.

This leader went on to command a brigade and serve as a Chief of Staff of the 82nd Airborne Division. I see him today in the corporate world, and he is still soft-spoken, effective, and always "aligned" with his organization's mission and core values.

In the next section, let's specifically address those things that cause stress, particularly that dysfunctional form of stress called "distress."

Causes of Distress: The First Cause of Stress

The first cause of stress in organizations: The *leader* knows something that the *people* don't know.

Imagine, if you will, that a leader has told his or her people to work on a project. This leader tells the people little about the project, other than it's very important to the leader, and the team needs to put their maximum effort into the project. However, the leader hasn't told the team that there will be a 20% funding cut, and that cut is the reason for the project.

The first reason for stress in this situation stems from the fact that the leader hasn't disclosed all the information to his or her people, and they feel as if they don't know everything that they need to know in order to give their maximum effort.

The team says to each other, "Why are we killing ourselves on this? Does the boss know how ridiculous this is? There are so many other more worthwhile things we could be doing. Why are we working on this pet project?"

In this situation, the boss could easily alleviate unnecessary stress by saying something like, "The reason I have you working so hard on this is…" If you give your people one little nugget of information, it can make all the difference. The light bulbs will go off in their heads, and they will be aligned on your "center line," devoting their maximum effort to it and focusing more effectively on the task at hand.

Again and again, leaders will instead look at their people and say, "No, you don't understand it! You're not getting me. You're not working on my priorities!"

When I debrief the leader after the meeting, I ask, "Does it strike you that your people are working really hard and not being able to give you what you want? Do you think you're telling them everything they need to know?"

The leader replies, "I told them everything I thought they needed to know!"

"Well, if that's the case," I reply, "these are really smart folks, and they're working really hard on this project, so why is your message not getting across? I see them working nights and weekends on this project. What is the reason you think things aren't going well?"

After I see a brief glimmer of understanding in the leader's eyes, I continue by asking a question: "What are all the critical things that your people need to know?"

As the leader starts running through the list of things out loud for me, the leader always gets to a point where he or she realizes an omission, something the leader forgot to explain to the team. The leader says, "Well, I forgot to tell them that, but it's not a big deal." Au contraire. It is a big deal! And when this leader implemented a new process that revealed a little more about the purpose of the project, the team worked with higher effectiveness and morale.

Are you giving your folks all the information they need? I often found when I gave my best employees or Soldiers important work to do, they didn't always want to come back into the boss, hat in hand, and say, "You know, boss, we didn't get it. We don't understand." The reason I most often heard is that they felt if they came back for clarification, they would be perceived as lacking the "right stuff."

So an important skill to acquire for your team's success lies in your ability to walk around. I found I had to get up off my tail and meet my people where they were. I needed to circle back around after they had wrestled with a task for a period of time and see how the "process" was proceeding.

I'd ask them, "How's it going?"

The first few times I visited them, they would say, "Everything is going fine, Sir," whether it really was or not.

However, after a few days or after the third or fourth time I walked around to visit my people, they opened up a little more: "Well, you know, Sir, we are actually struggling with this little piece here."

At that point, like the leader in my earlier example, I'd discover that I left a little piece out of my description. I would say, "Did I tell you _____?"

More often than not, the response was, "No, Sir, I don't believe you gave us that information, or if you did, it didn't sound like this when it got to us" (we were a bit "off" of the center line perhaps?).

At that point, I would explain that little piece of things, and why it was so important. The response was always positive at that point, and we all walked away with smiles on our faces: "Okay, now we understand. We can make this work." I know that my people would give me their maximum because they now knew how critical their work was. All it takes is consistently walking around, persistence, and a willingness to listen and to act on what you hear.

The Second Cause of Stress

The second cause of stress in organizations is the reverse of the first. It is as follows: The *people* know something that their *leader* doesn't know.

When your people sense that something is not working very well, does the work climate encourage them to go back to the boss and say, "This isn't working so well. How can we adjust in order to improve?"

It is hard to be viewed as a naysayer in an organization. There are usually countless people who will stand between a naysayer and the boss. He or she will hear things like, "This is the boss's pet project—don't mess with it!" or "Do you know how hard the boss has worked to make that happen?" or "That will be career suicide, man! Don't do it."

As a leader, what can you do to facilitate an environment where the truth actually does get back to you? It is extremely valuable to hear well-constructed criticism. For example, an employee might want to say, "I know this plan looked really good on a PowerPoint chart three weeks ago in the conference room, but now that we are trying to execute it out here on the ground, it's not going very well at all." Your people have to be able to tell you what's going on in real time.

Check Boxes

I thought I was pretty good at communicating with my team, having worked really hard at it over many years. I was good at being open, and I was good at taking criticism. If people came to me, I would do my best to listen. In 1993 I had an amusing (but troubling) wake-up call in the form of check boxes.

One of my duties was to oversee what we called the Review Process for all of the efficiency ratings we gave our Soldiers. Every person at the rank of Sergeant or above had a Rater to whom they directly reported, who in turn rated their performance. After that, there was a Senior Rater who would make sure that we talked about the Soldier's potential, and gave an appropriate and specific review of the Soldier.

After the Senior Rater was finished with his or her review, the forms would be sent along to me in my post as a Commander at the time. A good number of these forms crossed my desk for review.

The process of reviewing an efficiency report was relatively simple.

1. I would make sure each Soldier had the correct ratings because this rating would become part of that Soldier's official personnel file.

2. I would look at each Soldier's report in detail and the ratings that Soldier had been given in order to insure that there weren't any inconsistencies. For example, if the Rater said that one Soldier walked on water with Jesus Christ, and the Senior Rater said the same Soldier couldn't walk and chew gum at the same time, that would be a blunt inconsistency that I would flag and have to look into.

3. My job was to identify and resolve any such inconsistencies. At that point, I would usually bring in the Rater and the Senior Rater at the same time and say, "Explain these two inconsistencies to me."

Again, I worked hard to make sure that ours was a climate where folks could come and tell me when things were not working so well and to tell me the information I needed to know.

The efficiency report had a number of boxes. One of them was reserved for my mark, and I would check the box with a modest but clear checkmark (☑).

Every week, my people would bring in a stack of ten or twenty of these reports to me, and I would carefully look through each one and then I would check the box, sign my name, make sure everything was done to standard, and then send the reports on their way.

One day, there was a short-notice report that had to get into a Soldier's file right away, so the Sergeant came to me directly with the form. He stood in front of me and said, "Sorry to bother you, but no one else is here right now. I wouldn't have come directly in to see you, but we need to get this done in order to take care of this Soldier right away. Would you be able to look at this report and review it?"

I admired the Sergeant's tenacity, and I agreed. I told him, "Sure, bring the form here."

While he was standing there, I paged through the report, reviewing each page, and then saw that everything had been done to standard. I took my pen out, checked the box, and then signed my name.

As I was checking the box, however, I saw the Sergeant seize up and wince. It was a clear and visceral reaction to what I had done. I immediately asked him, "What's wrong?"

He said courteously, "Oh, nothing, Sir."

I said, "Your mouth says there's nothing wrong, but I watched your reaction when I signed this form, and all your non-verbal behaviors tell me that something is wrong. Would you please tell me what I did?"

At that point, the Sergeant shrugged again and repeated, "Oh, Sir, it's nothing."

I said, "Look, I'm telling you that it's something. Now, please tell me."

This discussion continued for longer than either of us would have liked, but I kept after him and I made him sit down until he finally looked at me, sighed, and said, "Sir, the problem is that when we take all these files to the central Personnel Action Center that processes these reports, if there's a check mark, they reject them."

I said, "Well, what do they want in there?"

He said, "Well, Sir, they want an x in the box (x), not a check mark."

With a look of surprise on my face, I said, "I've been doing these for four to five months now, and I have been sending out ten or more of these things a week. If I quickly do the math, at ten a week, I've sent out about 200 of these reports with a check mark in this box. What is going on?"

He grimaced and said, "Sir, it's OK. We have a bottle of White Out down in my office and when the reports come back from you, we have a Soldier who pulls them all out and puts White Out over your checkmark. Then I put an x in the box."

I responded with incredulity. "So you're telling me that we have a young Corporal who is sitting down there painting over my check marks, thinking that we have a stupid Colonel whom we can't tell to put an x in a box properly? We are pulling a Corporal away from his real job of taking care of Soldiers and writing up reports to basically filling in my checkmark and putting an x in the box?"

He said, "Yes, Sir, that's correct."

I said, "Why are we doing this?"

He said, "Well, Sir, I went to the Captain, who is in charge of all of this, and asked him to talk to you about this, and the Captain said you were too busy to be bothered with it, and we should just keep quiet and not bother you."

I couldn't believe what I was hearing. That Corporal was sitting in his office and every time he saw a file folder of reports coming down to me, he was sitting there saying to himself, "I know what I am going to have to do when those come back—White Out Boles' checkmarks! Why can't anyone just go and tell this stupid Lieutenant Colonel how to put an x in a box?"

I wasn't wedded to the check mark, and I would have been happy to put an x in the box if somebody had told me. I was upset at the time about the stress and all of the wasted time and effort that such a little box had caused. They used White Out over my checkmark, waited for it to dry, and then put an x neatly back in the box, so that the form wouldn't get thrown out before it got processed. I calculated that we probably spent an extra ten minutes on every report, and with 200 reports over the time I had made that error, that was 2,000 minutes we had wasted, all because nobody wanted to come in and tell me the truth.

Although that check box story happened nearly two decades ago, I still remember every detail of that day. I would have been fine putting an x in the box, but nobody bothered to tell me that. With all of the effort I had put into being accessible to my people and trying to be open, they still didn't feel comfortable telling me that I should put an x into a box instead of a checkmark.

The Right Climate

In the same way that you walk around to your people, so that you can find out whether you are disseminating the correct information to them, you also have to make sure that they are able to walk up to you and tell you things that make a difference within your organization, even if those things are as small as a checkmark.

Nearly all of my clients find this process the greatest challenge. Some of you reading this might say you are introverted, and such "walking around" doesn't come easy to you. I'm not too different, in a way. I don't like to go out and talk to big groups of people. My advice is to listen to your own needs, and in my case, that means I don't talk to big groups of people, but I do speak to smaller groups (and sometimes, I bite the bullet and do a large presentation).

All you need to do is create a climate of accessibility. Grab a cup of coffee or a can of soda, and walk around your organization. Stop in at a few desks, smile a little, and ask what's going on. It's not important that you speak—it's important that you listen.

If you have a tour guide or someone who wants to rush you through things, as if you are a presidential candidate going to a meet-and-greet, slow that guide down. Don't let that person rush you through meeting people. Take the time to shake hands. It will mean a lot to your people, no matter how big or small your organization is. Ask them what they are working on, and how you might be able to help.

The first few times you walk around like this, you will get boilerplate responses, but after a few times, as your people grow used to you, they will open up. From my experience, there is somebody out there who wants to talk with you about a checkmark and you REALLY need to hear it.

Remember Your Friends

As you become more senior and move up the leadership chain, you may find you have to force yourself to stay connected.

In 2002, I was in Kuwait on a visit, checking out our stocks that we were downloading and issuing in preparation for the invasion of Iraq. As I moved through the various offices between meetings and updates, I ran into an Officer with whom I had served eleven years earlier in Desert Shield/Desert Storm. I was a Major, and he was a Lieutenant then. Now I was a One-Star General and he was a Major. It was a pleasant surprise to see a familiar face from a special place in my memory, and we began to catch up: our spouses and his children (Cheryl had been the nurse when his wife was pregnant), recent assignments, and hobbies (he restored old cars). After a few minutes, his respectful demeanor changed. His responses became curt, his posture went from "at ease" to attention. I leaned in and asked what was wrong. He said, "Sir, do you know how many people are behind you right now looking daggers at me for keeping you from wherever you're headed next?" Sure enough—I turned around and the "parade" was in full view. There they were, a line of staffers checking on the young Major who was "wasting" the General's time while they were waiting after having laid waste to at least three trees to build the PowerPoint charts they were so anxious to brief me on.

Now, this Officer KNEW me. He had known me when I was a Major. He knew that I'd rather spend time with him than in a conference room suffering "death by PowerPoint." Because I was now a General Officer, to this Officer I was no longer the Major who had been known as "Uncle Vinny" to the young Lieutenants in Iraq. I was now "The General," who wasn't expected to have the time to be "bothered" with young Officers and their concerns anymore.

As you move up in leadership, you are responsible for staying connected with friends who knew you when you were working your way up. These friends may feel that your new responsibilities have made you "too important" and them "less important" to take up your time.

Keeping connected is not an easy undertaking. I found that having my phone book next to my phone and in a prominent place on my desk made it easier BEM (before email). Now, staying connected is easier with email, but I find I have to initiate the process by shooting those emails out. Also, I have to respond promptly when these friends reach out. It takes some effort, but the honest feedback from friends who know you is well worth the effort.

There will be some who will abuse your time. They are easily recognizable, and you can drop them from your lists of contacts. I have found them to be a minority.

TEN TAKEAWAYS

☆ ☆

1. Take the time to identify the "Center Line" for your team. What are the important norms, values, and behaviors that you want to permeate the organization?

2. How "aligned" is the team to this center line? Do you have mechanisms to disseminate and reinforce the norms, values, and behaviors? How do new people get exposed to the center line?

3. Stress is a given in your condition as a leader, and "bad" things happen to good teams and organizations. Great teams are defined by how well they respond to untoward events.

4. "Eustress" is the type of stress that encourages growth. It is akin to the stress inherent in muscle development or the development of your team.

5. "Distress" is dysfunctional and harder to address, yet more critical because its lingering is debilitating to you and the team.

6. Build your organization's adaptation to stress by engaging the stressors rather than ignoring them and "hoping" they leave. ("Hope" is not a viable course of action.)

7. Keep your team informed as a tool to reduce stress. ("I know something you don't know" isn't helpful.)

8. Stay open when work on a task is not going well, so your team can let you know, and you can fix the problem. (There is no shortage of "help" trying to keep bad news away from the boss.)

9. When you are surprised that a subordinate's performance is substandard, don't be surprised that their subordinates aren't surprised at the substandard performance. They will be surprised that you were surprised.

10. The higher you move up the executive chain of leadership, the harder you have to reach down and reconnect with those who knew you when you were moving up. Remember your friends.

THE SOLUTION
Finding Balance

*"Problems arise in that one has to find a balance
between what people need from you
and what you need for yourself."*

- Jessye Norman

We all do our best to establish a balance between work life and home life. It's always a struggle, especially a struggle for deployed Soldiers, who end up missing a whole bunch of activities with their families for weeks, months, or years at a time.

In 2007, the top deployment cycles were raised from twelve months to 15 months in both Iraq and Afghanistan. A well-intentioned civilian said at the time, "Well, it's only 90 more days—how bad could that be?"

I reminded that person that 15 months would be two Christmases, two missed birthdays, two Mother's Days, two seasons of dance recitals, two cycles of missing just about anything. It's one thing to tell a child, "Daddy has to miss this birthday, but he'll be there for the next one," and another thing entirely to have to say, "Daddy missed this birthday and he won't be there for the next one either."

Balance Isn't 50:50

Recently, I was invited to speak at Carson Newman College near Knoxville, Tennessee for an audience of 150-200 people as part of a lecture series about service to the nation.

The Officer who invited me to give the lecture had worked for me, and I had stayed in touch with him through the years. He was a great Soldier and then chose to return to college after he deployed to Iraq. He brought his family with him to Tennessee, so that he could attend Carson Newman.

My wife, Cheryl, knew what I would be doing that day, visiting various dignitaries and VIPs at the school, so she went out shopping with the Officer's wife, something they wouldn't have had time to do in the past when we had lived on the same base.

While the two women were having lunch and catching up, the Officer's wife said to Cheryl, "I haven't heard Vinny speak since we served together twelve years ago!"

My wife responded, "Well, let's go sneak in the back, and we can listen for a little while."

Up on stage, where I was standing and giving a presentation about the Army, what we were going through at the time, and how deployments were going, I happened to see my wife sneak in the back of the room, but she didn't notice that I saw her.

During the question and answer period, a young senior in college, a young cadet, about ready to become a Second Lieutenant, put up his hand and said, "Sir, I have a girlfriend, and we talk about balance a lot, including the stress of deployments, and how to make all this stuff happen." I was impressed by the young man's ability to open up in front of the audience.

I continued to listen. He said, "I'm just interested because you kind of talk about your real perspective about how you handle all of this." He was asking me a very difficult question. I probably should have expected that question, but I hadn't, and I was caught off guard.

As I stood in front of the audience, trying to figure out how to answer the question, I did what most speakers will do if they have a chance. I punted the ball!

I said, "I could give you my answer, but let's talk about somebody who could answer that question because she was always on the receiving end. Any time I was in or out of balance, and any time that I was stressed, my wife Cheryl would save the day."

I pointed my wife out to the crowd. To her surprise, I had seen her enter the room, and she was caught off guard. I said, "Cheryl, what would you say to that question?"

She grimaced a bit because she's an introvert at heart. Then she stood up, smiled at everybody, looked at me with daggers, as if to say, "You're going to get yours later!" and then proceeded to give the following beautiful answer.

"The first thing I had to understand about balance, being married to a Soldier, was that balance isn't 50:50. Balance is never even, and I found if I always tried to search for that, I'd always be disappointed. Instead, I see balance as understanding how much you have together. There were times that all he could give me was five or ten percent. His unit would be getting ready to deploy, or something would come up in training and he would be really engaged, committed, and dedicated to that. I would have to treasure the ten percent of his time that he could give me."

She said it also sometimes works the other way. "When he had plenty of time, and had just gotten back from deployment, he would have 90 percent of his time to give me. Boy, sometimes it was harder to have 90 percent than it was to have ten percent!" This got the room laughing. I enjoyed being the punch line of Cheryl's gentle joke.

She continued, "In all seriousness, I only want about 30 to 50 percent of my husband's attention, but sometimes he would want to give me the entire 90 percent, so I would have to figure out how to balance that all out."

The Balance We Want

My wife had rescued me from a difficult place in my speech and done a brilliant job! But I also learned a great deal from what she said that day.

The key takeaway that I took from Cheryl's insight was that balance is an elusive goal. If you always want to have a 50:50 balance between work and your job, you will be disappointed because many times, the best you're going to get is ten percent. This doesn't just go for people in the military. It goes for anyone with a pulse.

Sometimes you will give your job 90 percent and only have ten percent for your family. The important thing is that sometimes you will also have 90 percent for your family. Make sure that it always averages out. That's the best that most of us can hope for.

While she was speaking to the audience on that day, Cheryl made this critical point. She said, "Even if it was only ten percent, I needed that small percentage of his time. I would not share that small bit of time with anything else. So, put down your BlackBerry, put down your laptop, put down your other things. If all you can give is ten percent, by God make sure that you give everything to that ten percent."

A hush fell over the room when she made her last point. "That is really the balance we want. We don't want more than what you have to give. Just give us everything you can, and we will use that, take strength from that, and grow."

Balancing Act

My wife used to hate when I'd say once a week, "Let's sit down and do a calendar scrub for the next six to eight weeks."

However, after a while, she came to realize that if we sat down and spent that time together, I could convey to her when I would be working and at what capacity, so that she could be prepared and not surprised by my varied schedule.

I found that it can be a great tool to use your calendar as a forcing function and do calendar scrubs. Try talking with your spouse and to your family, and show them how a balancing act could work. Tell them, "Next week I will be able to spend ten percent of my time with you, but the week after that, I'll have 40 percent of my time to spend. Could we plan some fun events for that week together?" There is great strength in openness.

Some time ago, I worked for a Three-Star General in Fort Hood, Texas. We were in the middle of a simulation exercise on a Friday evening when the General looked up and said, "You better hurry up and be done in the next half hour because I have to go to headquarters and change."

Several people responded, "Sir, what do you have to change for?" He didn't reply right away.

Somebody finally asked him, "Sir, we didn't know you had another briefing after this. What do you have to go change for? Do you have a VIP thing? Do you have to put your dress uniform on? What do you have to do?"

The General said, "No, I have to go put my civilian clothes on. My kid is going to play football tonight."

Smiling like a proud father, he continued, "I don't miss a football game if I'm off."

At that moment, many of us realized that the whole notion of balance was something we could attain and achieve, even if we reached the highest rungs of leadership in our job.

Family is important to work, and work is important to family. In fact, oftentimes work improves as a direct result of family. Imagine the great leaders in history without the people around them who cared for them and advised them in times of need.

Some of the great leaders I have watched over the years want to know not only when their people's birthdays are, but also when the spouse's birthday is. Why?

As a leader, you can see the positive effects when you send the spouse a birthday card saying, "I want to thank you for all the great support you've given to your husband/wife. I just want to thank you for everything you do because it really makes a difference to this organization."

All of a sudden, on the spouse's birthday, go up to your employee and say, "We usually let you take an extra hour, an afternoon, or a day off when it's your birthday. Well, why don't you take half a day off when it's your spouse's birthday? Get out of here and go take your spouse to lunch or dinner."

You'd be surprised how that one balancing act by a leader makes all the difference in the world.

The Balance Equation

The best measure of balance is how you feel about how you are using your time. From an equation perspective I think it looks like the following:

$$B \; f \; 24 \; I/U$$

Balance (B) is a function (f) of the 24 hours in a day and what part of the 24 hours you spend on important things (I) vs. urgent things (U).

Urgent Things

These are things you have to ensure that someone in the organization is doing and that you are tracking that person (not micromanaging) to validate that those things are getting done.

Important Things

These are things only *you* can do. Only you can evaluate your direct reports (try to have your assistant do it and watch how that works out). Only you can be the dad at your son's recital or your daughter's soccer game. Only you can take your wife out on Valentine's Day.

Leaders who want to lead and demonstrate a balanced work-life model for their folks should review their calendars and assess their time usage. Are you spending it on tasks that are urgent vs. important?

You'll show an ability to function at a high level for your team when you recognize that you get paid to do your job and the *important* duties that entails, not someone else's job. That includes at home and at work.

TEN TAKEAWAYS

☆ ☆

1. Balance isn't 50/50. It is giving what you can when you can.

2. People like avoiding responsibility when they say, "I gave it to the boss" (now you are working for them).

3. Make important vs. urgent a mantra as you scan your calendar.

4. You conduct calendar scrubs at work to ensure you don't miss important things. Do it at home so you don't miss those important things.

5. Say "No" when you get asked to do something that is not yours to do (pick your spot).

6. You define your balance. There were people who didn't understand what the big deal was with the move from 12- to 15-month deployments. They had to be educated.

7. Balance won't mean the absence of stress or pain. Balance means you can handle the stress and the pain.

8. Taking time for yourself isn't a crime to be ashamed of. It's a virtue to take care of yourself.

9. You need to read, think, eat and exercise every day. You have to make the time. As you go up the ladder, there will be no one to force you to take care of yourself.

10. "God only asks of you the strength you possess. The only thing that is impossible is to run away," from a speech by Liv Ulman in Berlin, Germany, 1985 at an award presentation by the International Red Cross for her charitable work in Africa.

ONE NON-NEGOTIABLE
Trust

TRUST
The Most Critical Component

*"To be trusted is a greater
compliment than being loved."*

- George MacDonald

I believe that the ultimate validation of one's leadership abilities can be measured by the willingness of individuals to place their trust in that leader. Will they suspend their judgment and instincts for yours? Will they, as MacDonald states in the quote on the previous page, feel that you, as their leader, have created a partnership with those you lead?

The absence of that willingness leads to a gap between the leader and the led. That gap diminishes the capability of a team or organization to attain excellent results and applies not only to the organization as a whole, but also to the people in that organization.

Leaders have to make the effort to build the climate of trust, which brings value added to your business outcomes. And trust is a hot topic. A Google search of the phrase "statistics on trust in the workplace" generates 124,000,000 hits. Given all this information and statistics, we might assume trust is common in the workplace, but the great value of trust can be measured by its scarcity.

A highly regarded tool for measuring trust is the Edelman Trust Barometer, which has been conducted and published for well over a decade by the Daniel J. Edelman Holdings Group. The barometer assesses trust around the world in terms of business, government, non-governmental organizations (NGOs), and the religious denominations of the various countries. In the 2013 release, the barometer surveyed over 31,000 consumers in 26 countries between the ages of 25 and 64.

What were the results? The barometer found that fewer than one in five respondents believe that a "business or government leader will actually tell the truth when confronted with a difficult issue."

That means that out of a population of over 31,000, fewer than 6,200 people believe a leader will be truthful when the times are tough.

A blog posting entitled "Three Reasons I Care About Trust" by Alan Vandermolen, Vice Chairman of the Daniel J. Edelman Holdings Group, accompanied the roll-out of the 2013 trust barometer. Vandermolen states that "Trust is a leading indicator." Specifically, it is "how you are perceived to behave in the future. If stakeholders grant trust to companies, those companies have permission to lead."

If the market perceives you are worthy of trust, especially when trust is in such short supply, it falls to reason that the market grants a competitive advantage to those who possess trust.

Edelman's trust barometer encapsulated the essence of trust into five clusters:

> **1. Engagement** — Is there transparency in the organization? Is there care for employees and customers?
>
> **2. Integrity** — Is it visible? Do leaders "walk their talk"?
>
> **3. Quality Products and Services** — Does the organization make or provide something they are proud to stand for and stand behind?
>
> **4. Purpose** — Does the organization make the greater society better instead of using only a financial equation for validation of its purpose?
>
> **5. Operations** — Specifically, do the leaders conduct themselves honorably? Is the company viewed as being at the top of their industry category?

It is hard to argue with any of these criteria as a fulcrum upon which to leverage an organization's trust quotient.

Given the scarcity of trust, why do leaders in government and business find it so difficult to bridge that gap between themselves and their people's willingness to trust their leaders? Here are a few of my reasons:

- **People have been "burned"** by leaders in their past trust experiences, which heightens their resistance to trust in the future.

- **It is hard to measure**. Trust is viewed as a "touchy feely" objective. For example, how would you write a performance objective that measured the level of trust that the leader attained from the led?

- **Leaders find it difficult to do**. They have to establish a climate of trust. That means letting people make mistakes and ensuring they learn from them. The leader has to let go of some of the control/power they perceive they have: "If I already know how to do it, why take the risk of letting you try it?"

- **Trust is personal**. Individuals have their own personal trust equation or logic trail they follow to confer trust in another. Some do it more willingly than others; however, you cannot assume because some seem to trust you that all do.

- **Trust is easily lost**. My experience has shown me that if a leader violates the bond of trust with the led, even once, that trust will be gone and not easily regained. Because it's personal, people feel personally violated when trust is breached.

Let me expand on some of these points.

When people have been burned in their past trust experiences, this event really becomes critical if it happens to somebody at a very young stage in their career: young Lieutenants, young Seargents, young Captains, new first-line employees who are put in a management position. If these people trust a leader and get burned by trusting that superior, a few reactions set in. The young person who was burned may say, "That's the way the system works," or "You've got to look out for yourself," or "You better protect yourself because nobody's going to take care of you but you."

If a leader fails someone in the organization who is at a very seminal, impressionable point in his or her professional life, that failure of trust has an overriding effect on the rest of that person's development. Whenever people who have been burned early on want to trust an experience, a superior, or somebody else, they always have that little feeling in their back that says, "I don't know about this..." If those people don't work through that feeling and overcome it, then those people become the naysayers in an organization.

People don't just get burned by a failure of trust; it gets burned into them that they trusted a leader and their trust was wrong. These people then overreact and overcompensate by saying, "I'm not going to trust anybody again." Maslow's hierarchy of needs places self-actualization at the top, and that's what you need to achieve in order to maximize your returns on relationships. But if you get to a level where you're never going to trust somebody because you got burned once before, then you're going to be a prisoner of that experience, and you'll never be able to expand beyond that imprisonment.

Another reason that the willingness to trust is a hard gap to bridge is because leaders find establishing trust hard to do. First of all, trust is not about management. Trust is about leadership. And a lot of what I see that passes for leadership really are attempts at management: "I am managing a task. You people are butts on the rowing bench, and your only question is whether the captain wants to go waterskiing or just wants to go for a ride. So my job is to manage you to a task. It is not to lead you, or develop you, or put you in a position where you can take my job some day. It's none of that. It's just that I'm going to manage a task list, and you're an instrument." If you are a leader who believes that the personal resources given to you are simply resources to accomplish tasks, then you're not going to be inclined to trust individuals or even concern yourself with the trust equation. You're going to say, "I don't need to worry about trust. I'm the boss. That's all I need to know. You don't like it? When you get to be the boss, you can do something different." Those kinds of conversations are legion and illustrate why leaders find establishing a climate of trust so difficult to do.

When a leader trusts somebody, he or she also has to let go of a little power. When I let go of power and trust you to do something, I can't stand over you every 15 seconds. I've got to trust that you can accomplish the task. And I've got to trust myself that I've made the right decision, so that when you accomplish the task, everything works out well. But I also have put enough flex into the equation that when things don't work out well, we can sort things out, recover from the situation, and move on.

As a leader, I have to not only trust those I lead, I have to trust my own judgment, and I have to get into the habit of trusting my own judgment in order to make decisions. How do I decide whether or not to trust? I tend to do a best-thing, worst-thing comparison. What's the best thing that will happen if I trust this person? The best thing is that everything will work out, the person will feel empowered, things are going to get done, and that's pretty positive. What's the worst thing that will happen? The worst thing is that I'm going to have to do some work at the end putting everything back together again and reviewing the situation carefully. The real key here isn't if something fails or not; the real key is how you react to that person's mistake. Do you kick them in the rear end and say, "Well, I knew you couldn't do it anyway" and beat them down forever. Or do you put your arm around that person and say, "Hey, come on. How do we need to fix this?" When you involve the person in the solution, everything improves.

The last point I make about the difficulty of bridging that gap of trust is that trust is so perishable. It is very, very easy to lose. You may have a year or two of positive experiences building trust, but if you act in a distrustful way, you will lose those two years of work. Because leaders can lose trust overnight, they may be reluctant to trust and might say, "Well, I'm not going to put myself out there" or "I'm not going to trust somebody unless I really, really, really, really know them." That's like saying I'm not going to trust my wife until I'm really, really, really, really sure I can trust her. How long does that take? Let's say you've been married twenty years — are you there yet? With this kind of attitude, it's also easy to develop a habit of not trusting, and leaders may end up just doing the basics in their job while also relying more on themselves than on anyone else.

First off, I will say that more often than not, I trusted people and it worked out. So when I trusted somebody and it didn't work out, that was a unique experience for me. Part of that is luck. Part of that is experience and judgment. When I was much younger, I had to be much more careful, but as I continued in my career, I got pretty good about reading folks and making a decision about whom I could trust and not trust. I also made a decision about gradations of trust. I might trust you with a B-team issue first and see how you handled that if we had time. Then I'd trust you with another

B-team issue, and then I'd trust you with an A-team issue, and things would start to work out.

When I did trust someone and the situation did not work out, I had to fight the urge to get mad at myself. When I got mad at myself, I'd beat myself up for a while, and when I finally got over that initial reaction, I had to then focus on why things hadn't worked out. Sometimes, I chose poorly. I thought somebody could handle my trust, but they proved me wrong. This kind of situation can be painful and can turn bitter. To this day, I'm sure that if you mention my name to some people, they will be disgusted because they feel that "Boles didn't understand." In those cases, I reviewed the situation, looked at it in my heart, and I believed I assessed the situation about as right as I could. I gave the person a break, an opportunity to get it right, and that person didn't get it right. I didn't check on the person enough, and that's my fault. But I won't make that same mistake with that person again.

Just as it's easy for a leader to lose trust, so too is it easy for a member of an organization to lose a leader's trust. If someone loses my trust, I tend to sit down with that person and ask, "What happened? What went wrong?" Some people continue to ignore the opportunity to build trust again and might say, "Well, Sir, the problem is that you just don't understand." My response tends to be, "OK, you work for me, and I thought I understood this situation pretty well, and now it's my fault. OK, wait a minute." Then I review the situation again and if I find the person is still at fault, I say, "No. I don't think so. I think the ball's still in your court. It's still on you." If the person still resists taking responsibility, I then have to move on. That's difficult to say and hard to do, but it's necessary.

My most powerful lessons on trust in my leadership journey stem from my experience working as the aide for the greatest leader I ever saw, General John Mitchell, who was the U.S. Commander of Berlin when I worked for him for two years from 1984 to 1986. I was a Captain with just under ten years of experience in the Army, and I thought I had the Army by the tail and had everything figured out. With General Mitchell, I saw up close and personal from a senior leader what leadership and trust were all about. Mitchell was the most competent and confident leader I ever saw. When he trusted you, the good news was that he trusted you. The bad news was that he trusted you, and he trusted you completely and implicitly. If you failed, there was no way to categorize the depth of your despair.

By 1984, I had had a pretty easy time of it in the Army for a few reasons. I liked what I was doing in the Army. I also knew that being in the Army prevented me from working for my dad and the family business, something I did not want to do. I also enjoyed a significant degree of sucess at my level and age and was recognized by superiors for doing well. I kept getting thrown into jobs that some considered really difficult, and I kept doing those jobs well.

It's important to remember that in 1984, Berlin was still a divided city and the Wall was only 23 years old. Berlin was a massive city — large enough to fit Frankfurt, Stuttgart, and Munich within its borders and still be able to add a city the size of Washington D.C. Berlin was divided into sectors administered by the U. S., France, Britain, and the Soviet Union. The U. S. sector was the largest, and we had six of the city's burroughs. The other Allies viewed us not as the only dog but certainly as the lead dog.

The incident I'm about to tell was one in which I thought things were not going to work out.

General Mitchell's father had been a commissioner for the Social Security Administration under Harry Truman. Because of the General's knowledge of the political process and political figures, Mitchell became good friends with the American Ambassador to Germany, Arthur Burns. Burns knew Berlin and the history, and he and his wife enjoyed visiting the city and the General and his wife. Their get-togethers were wonderful events with lots of engaging talk.

It was time for the Ambassador to depart Berlin, and we had a big parade after which everyone was going to the train station. My job was to make sure that the boss, General Mitchell, was where he was supposed to be. The Ambassador was going to take a U. S. government train called a duty train (we called it the Ambassador's train) back to Bonn, and I told General Mitchell that we needed to be at the train station by 12:45 because the train was supposed to pull up at about 1:15. We arrived minutes before 12:45, and the boss's deputy stood at the station with an ashen look on his face. The deputy said, "The Ambassador's already on the train."

My boss looked at me and said, "What?" I told him I didn't know what happened, and the General and his wife ran on the train. The Ambassador didn't give their lateness a second thought, and they all had a wonderful farewell.

But the boss had wanted to be at the station to welcome the Ambassador, escort him on the train, get him settled, and see him off.

After the train pulled away, the crowd dispersed, and the band packed up, we got in the car to return, and the boss said in a very clipped tone, "Vinny, I want you to find out who messed this up."

I said, "Sir, I got it. I'm all over this. I will dig into this, and I will find out." I knew how important this event was to the General. Folks were supposed to keep me informed, and I had planned everything. I dropped the boss off at the house, went back to the office, and dug through the paper work. I got to a sheet of paper and discovered that I had missed a change to the schedule; the Ambassador was going to arrive at 12:30 and the train would pull in early. And I had missed that.

So now, here I was. I accomplished the boss's task. I found out who screwed up. The bad news is I have to look in a mirror to talk to the person who screwed up. So I picked up the phone, called the boss, and said, "Sir, you asked me to look into that problem, and I found out who messed it up." The boss asked me who the person was, and I said "Well, Sir, it was me. There was a schedule change, and I missed it. I didn't get back to the office to pick it up." There was a pregnant pause on the other end of the phone, and I said to myself, "OK, this isn't going to end well." I knew how important this event was to the General.

General Mitchell started chuckling and then said, "Well, Vinny. You don't normally screw things up too much. I'd appreciate it if you wouldn't do this again."

That one instance reinforced to me how important it was to trust people. General Mitchell trusted me. He did the balancing act and said, "You know, 9,999 times I give Vinny something and he makes it happen. We have one thing screw up, and I'm not going to cut somebody off because of that." As Shakespeare once said, "The quality of mercy is not strained," and I was blessed by General Mitchell's quality of mercy and trust.

One more story with General Mitchell demonstrates the lessons I learned about trust from this great leader. In 1986, the phone rang one Saturday morning, and the boss said, "Vinny, Vladimir Horowitz, the pianist, and his wife, Madam Toscanini, are coming. They're in Berlin, and I'd like to have them for dinner, and I'd like to have the Ambassador come to dinner, too."

I said, "Well, very good, Sir. I can make that happen. When is it?"

General Mitchell said, "I'd like to do it tonight."

I said, "OK, Sir" and gulped a little bit because this event would be tough to pull off on such short notice.

The boss then said, "Now, Vinny, you've got to work this very delicately because Horowitz will agree to come if he knows the Ambassador is attending, and the Ambassador will attend if he knows Horowitz is coming."

"Sir, I understand. They'll be fine," I said. "Well, Sir, would you tell me where Horowitz is staying?"

Mitchell said, "I don't know." So here I was in Berlin, a city of millions of people, and I had to find out where Vladimir Horowitz was staying — not information people generally wanted to give right up. My German was terrible — not good enough to call the Philharmonie and say, "Excuse me. I'd like you to tell me where Horowitz is staying." I also knew that I could not get a lot of people involved because if the word got out that the boss was having dinner with Horowitz, I would be besieged by people who wanted to be on the guest list.

I called my Hausmeister, who ran the house for us and I said, "Erhard, what can I do?" Erhard knew several people in the inner workings of the host reception business, and he immediately gave me the phone number of the concierge at the Kempinksi hotel.

Erhard said, "Sir, I think Horowitz would stay at the Kempinski, but if he's not staying at the Kempinski, the concierge will tell you what you need. The concierge knows you from the times he's worked here on some functions."

When I reached the concierge, he recognized me, and after I told him what I needed, he asked me, "Sir, would you like to speak to Horowitz's aide?" The concierge immediately patched me upstairs, I got Horowitz's aide on the phone, and quickly explained what we were trying to do.

The aide said, "All right. Call you right back." He called me back and said, "Maestro will be happy to come to dinner. Here's what he likes to eat. He likes to eat early at four when he's performing. He's not performing tonight but would like to keep that routine."

I said, "OK. I got it."

Now, when people around me have heard this story, they say, "I wouldn't know where to turn. I wouldn't know what to do. I wouldn't know where to start." Because I knew General Mitchell trusted me, that galvanized me to accomplish a difficult task. There's an old phrase — "Don't take counsel of your fears" — and I refused to take counsel of any fears. I knew Mitchell wanted me to get this task done, he was counting on me, and I was going to make that event happen if I had to move heaven and earth to do it. I was just going to do it.

After speaking with Horowitz's aide, I called the Amabassador's aide, and received a confirmation that the Ambassador and his wife would be able to attend. Then I called Erhard and explained what we needed. Erhard said, "Not a problem. But we're going to have one small issue. For this dinner party of seven to eight people, the entire house staff will be working."

I said, "Erhard, we don't need the whole house staff for such a small dinner party."

Erhard said, "Sir, if you think I'm going to have Horowitz in this house and then pick and choose who will get to work, that's impossible. The whole staff will attend."

I said, "I got it. I understand."

Horowitz's aide called with the menu, which was a sole dish, a potato pancake, and some kind of fruit tart. Erhard explained to the chef, George, what we needed. After dinner, Horowitz tried to convince George to work for him. And we had a wonderful evening. Mrs. Mitchell was an accomplished artist, so she did a quick painting of Horowitz on the cover of Time magazine, which featured Horowitz, and the pianist signed the cover, "The Maestro."

This was one of those world-class, phenomenal evenings. But that's not the point. General Mitchell thought nothing of picking up the phone and saying, "Vinny, go figure this out." Mitchell trusted me to get the almost-impossible done. Because I knew he trusted me, I was galvanized to succeed. I am a good example of how folks will accomplish great things if their leaders trust them. My years as General Mitchell's aide were a great learning experience in leadership. I had just under ten years in the Army, but those years with Mitchell reinforced the ways I trusted people and worked with them over the next 23 years as I continued to move into higher leadership positions.

Just as General Mitchell trusted me implicitly, I also have trusted many completely. But I have also experienced times when I've used the best-thing, worst-thing comparison and concluded, "This project is too important for it not to work. I have to be involved in this task more fully." Then I'd tell the people working for me, "Look, I'm going to be more involved than normal in this project because we are only going to get one shot at this. We're only going to get one time to do it right."

One example occurred at the national training center in Fort Irwin, California, and we were given the challenging task to drive 5,000-gallon fuel tankers over a new piece of terrain in the mountainous desert. With good reason, California has its own rather restrictive environmental rules, so a spilling of a 5,000-gallon tanker with about 4,500 gallons worth of fuel on it would make for a significant event. Normally, I would have told my team, "Hey, you've got a new route. You've picked an experienced convoy to accomplish this task. Go ahead." But I told my team, "This is a route we've never done before. I need to be out there watching this mission."

To this day, I recall the pride and joy I felt watching my team take off and accomplish the task. They acted as if I weren't there; they just moved out and did what they had been asked to do.

When we went over the project afterwards, some people who had observed us said, "We didn't think you could drive those tankers over that terrain." And my kids' attitude was, "We knew we were going to do this. We just knew we were going to make this happen." They accomplished a difficult task because I trusted them. But I also had to "grade their homework real close," as a boss once said. As a leader, you have to decide when you must grade your team's homework real close or not.

So let's visit the next and most pertinent question: How do we get an organization into a trusting environment?

A combination of my review and experience led me to "Building Trust in the Workplace," an article published online in 2007 by Deb Clifford of Inspired People. Clifford lists five trust-building behaviors:

1. **Promise only when you are positive**: Don't promise based on what you think, but on what you know for sure. Once a promise is out there, you can't take it back easily.

2. **When you don't have an answer, say so. And then find one:** The team doesn't expect you to know everything about everything all the time. But if they care enough to ask, they want to have a leader who cares enough to get the right answer.

3. **Tell the truth as much as you can as fast as you can:** Bad news does not get better as it ages and in the absence of information, especially in today's 24/7/365 connected world, your team will be inundated with rumors and falsehoods. So get the information out. As you do, be sensitive to the fact that, in my experience, initial reports are at best 50% accurate. As an old Sergeant once shared with me, "Truth on the battlefield has a date stamp."

4. **Don't say one thing and mean another:** Walk your talk. Enough said.

5. **When you ask for feedback—circle back:** When you ask someone to invest his or her time and energy to providing a suggestion, it's only fair to let that person know what use you made of the feedback. That person will appreciate your comments and will be willing to offer feedback again.

Clifford's five trust-building behaviors really came through to me in the summer of 2002. We were told to begin downloading our ships of pre-position materials in Kuwait and do it over a period of time. Our intelligence had told us that Saddam Hussein reacted by putting people on alert every time a ship was downloaded. So if we dragged the download out over a few months, Hussein would have a whole lot of people who weren't getting a whole lot of sleep.

We initially began this download with a workforce that wasn't up to the task. My folks had to come up with workarounds and other solutions. We had worked together since 9-11, and they knew how important each project was, so they knew to promise something only when they were positive. They knew not to come to me with a promise and say, "Sir, I'll do it by Wednesday" if they knew they couldn't accomplish the task until Thursday. Some people want to be optimists all the time, but I'm a fan of those who underpromise and overdeliver. I like the person who says, "I'll give it to you Thursday" and gives it to me Wednesday over the person who says they'll give it to me Thursday, and then I have to understand why I can't get it until Friday or Monday. As Clifford says, once a promise is out there, you can't take it back.

My folks also knew that when they didn't have an answer, they could tell me. When we had a project that involved a workforce that wasn't up to the task, my folks could have immediately started wringing their hands saying, "You know, this is awful. This is just awful." Instead, we said, "Look. This option isn't working. What's our next option?" We shifted the energy from focusing on the problem to finding an answer. That shift allowed us to find a great option that worked superbly. I pressed my folks to get not just any answer but to find the right answer.

Clifford also suggests telling the truth as much as you can as fast as you can. I've learned every day that bad news doesn't get better with age. However, I often think that the reason bad news doesn't get better with age is because of how leaders react to bad news. If you throw things around the room, then you'll be the type of leader who won't get a lot of bad news because your folks won't risk your reaction. If your leader is the type to react badly to bad news, you still have to deliver that bad news, much as I did with General Mitchell, when I picked up the phone and told him I had made a mistake. As a deliverer of bad news, you have to walk into your boss's office, deliver the news, and wait out the explosion. Then be calm enough to say, "OK, now that you've let out that reaction, we've got to work through this problem. What are we going to do?"

You have to tell the truth as much as you can. As Colin Powell said, "You're never going to get 100% of the facts all the time." And as one sergeant shared with me, you're not going to get 100% of the truth all the time.

Truth has a date stamp, especially on the battlefield. Truth evolves and changes. What was true today — "I had all the fuel I was supposed to have, I had all the equipment I was supposed to have" — that's not going to be true tomorrow unless we work at it.

The last trust-building behavior Clifford lists is to circle back when you ask for feedback. I've been in forums where the boss says, "Hey, give me your feedback. What do you think we should do." Everybody offers feedback, the boss processes it, and we all get up and leave. A few days later the boss makes a decision, but the folks who have given the feedback never find out about the decision. When a leader circles back and says, "Here's what I decided and why," then the folks in the organization know they have been heard.

In one instance, I disagreed with my boss. I told him, "Listen, Sir, I hear you, but I disagree." My boss said, "Yeah, I know. But that's what we're going to do." The boss went on to execute his plan, and things did not work out well. I didn't rub his nose in it. He had given me a chance to be heard. But I'll never forget that he circled back to me. He was a General Officer and I was a Major; there were four or five levels between our positions. This boss had never been to my office, but he drove down to my office, walked in, put his feet up on my desk, and said, "I screwed that one up. I really screwed that one up. I should have listened to you."

A Lesson Learned the Hard Way

Early in my career, when I had about five years in the Army and was assigned to my first command duty, an investigator called and asked to come see me about a matter his group was looking into.

Upon the investigators' arrival, I was informed that one of my Soldiers was suspected of being involved in a romantic relationship with a member of the same sex. The investigators expressed their concern about possible security problems. (Note: This was long before either the "Don't ask, don't tell" policy enacted in the early days of the Clinton administration or the now accepted [2012] policy of allowing gay service members to be open regarding their sexual orientation.)

I was asked to have the Soldier report to the investigators' offices and to only inform her that she might be able to help the investigators with their concern. The investigators intended to spring the surprise accusation on the unsuspecting Soldier. I was uncomfortable doing this, so I reached out for some counsel from senior leaders. I was told in essence, "Trust the professionals. Make the call."

Many hours later, I went to pick the Soldier up. The Soldier had made no admissions and denied the story; however, I felt sick at what I had done. We were teammates and I hadn't held up my end. I could rationalize my action behind the "system," but it wasn't right.

The investigation died, and we made no mention of it. A few weeks later, I was the victim of a false accusation, and the investigating system took a great deal of time to review the matter and exonerated me. One of the reasons I was exonerated was that the Soldier whom I had let down was a witness. And that Soldier told the investigating officer that I was to be trusted. If I said an event hadn't happened, then it hadn't.

I have never forgotten that I got more from that Soldier than I ever gave and never again did I ever, ever reach for expediency at the expense of trust.

Trust and ethics are personal. You have to be comfortable with your decisions, and if you're not comfortable, something is wrong. What I learned from that event early in my career was that I let my discomfort about ethics get overridden by saying, "Well, my boss told me it's OK, so it must be OK." I abrogated my professional responsibility, my trust to that officer over to the idea that the boss said it's OK.

I was young then, in my first duty assignment, and my boss had a high regard for me. I can see very easily how I may have said to myself, "No big deal." But I learned to treat people in my organization differently, so that if they were uncomfortable with something I proposed, I never tried to railroad them into it. If I had at all the capability, I would take the time to say, "What do I have to do to get you to be comfortable with this? I think it's necessary to do, but if you're not comfortable with it, you're not going to do it. So what do I have to do to make you comfortable with this?"

Sometimes, the reluctant person would say, "Sir, I don't know. Sir, I've got to think about it a little bit more." And I'd give that person the time to think. In the case of that Soldier's investigation, I let the investigative process and my boss's high regard of me color the entire situation. Looking back, I could have said to the investigative team, "Look, if you want to pick up the phone and call that Soldier and bring her in, knock yourself out. But I'm not pulling this little game to make you guys feel better." At a very young age, I learned the value of trust, how personal trust and ethics are, and how critical it is to retain trust. What I've learned over time is that I'm the only one who can worry about my trust.

I have ended this book on leadership with a chapter on trust, the most critical component. Some might say that I've overemphasized this critical component and that you don't really have to trust leaders — you just have to respect them. This statement is both fair and lacks something.

When you begin working for a leader, you owe them respect and obedience — respect for their position and obedience to what they tell you to do. But for a leader, the other things — confidence, competence, trust — those things don't just click on when you first work with an organization, especially if you have an experienced workforce. They'll sit there and say, "Yeah. OK. You're the sixth boss we've had, and yeah, we're all just bowing and trusting you." They will respect you and obey you; they owe you that. If they don't respect and obey you, they won't respect your position, and they've probably forfeited their right to stay in the organization.

Leaders must earn everything else besides respect and obedience — trust, confidence, candor — you have to earn these, and you have to earn them every day by your behavior. If you say to your workforce, "I want you to be honest and open and up front with me," then your people will ask, "OK, are you going to rip my head off when I tell you something you don't want to hear?" If you act counter to what you state, you will not gain that trust, confidence, and candor.

Leaders must ask themselves, "How do I mirror the behaviors I want? How do I show my people I'm the type of leader worthy of trust, confidence, and candor?" These qualities are very personal for each individual in your organization.

If we say we don't have to trust leaders, we just have to respect them, this is similar to saying that in a marriage, we don't have to trust the other partner; we just have to respect and obey that person, stay with that person, and don't ask the difficult questions that reveal the presence or lack of trust. You can do that, but something will always be missing. Something will always prevent the relationship or the performance from being all it can be. When people are trusted by their leaders, those people move the organization forward. When they're not trusted by their leaders, those people will have one eye looking forward and one eye looking back over their shoulder; they will always wonder if there's something else they need to be worried about.

This book claims that if you follow the recipe of 4-3-2, you will achieve 1, or trust, the one critical component for leaders. Is it possible to cut corners with this recipe? Can you achieve trust without one ingredient?

Anything is possible, but I have not seen leadership that deals with trust successfully unless that leadership has attended to all components. Each of the components builds on the other. If folks don't know how you're structured, and every day is discovery learning with the boss, they're not going to trust you. If you don't help them manage the critical relationships, if you just throw projects at them and say, "It's awful to be you. But you better get that done. And I don't really care who you have to piss off in order to get that task done," they're not going to trust you. If you don't help your people balance and mitigate risk by bringing your judgment to bear, they won't trust you. If your people take a risk and make a mistake, and you berate them for it and don't help them invest in the solution, they're not going to trust you. If you don't make decisions, they're certainly not going to trust you because that's really what leaders get paid to do. If you don't give your people a standard and a system, identify what they're in charge of or who's in charge, assign them a task and then not hold anyone accountable, they're not going to trust you. If you don't tell them the information they need and you don't listen to the information they pass to you, then you might have people who trust you, but they'll trust you only a little bit. They might say, "Well, he got seven out of ten. Good. I'll trust him seven out of ten times" or "Well, he's about four out of ten. I'll trust him four out of ten times." Which four? The person will say, "I don't know. I don't know which four." But we can be sure those four times won't be the first four the leader needs.

Anything's possible, but I have not yet seen a leader gain trust without paying close attention to the four expectations the team has of that leader, without asking and answering the three important questions, or without identifying and dealing with the two kinds of stress. As I said at the start of this book, the lessons of leadership are easily disseminated. But leadership is difficult, complex, and personal. Traveling the journey of leadership means respecting the long haul.

TEN TAKEAWAYS

☆ ☆

1. Trust may be given to you easily, but you can also lose it easily and for a long, long time.

2. Trust can be a competitive advantage because there is a scarcity of it.

3. Your people listen to what you say. They believe what they see you do.

4. Trust is personal. People have varying levels of comfort in conferring trust. If someone is burned early in a profession, that person will not trust easily.

5. You build the trust relationship every day.

6. If you ask folks to invest in the trust relationship, keep them informed with how it's going.

7. Trust is non-negotiable. There are no degrees of trust.

8. Bad news does not age well. Get the word out and keep putting it out. There is always someone who didn't get the word the first time.

9. In the absence of truth from you, the workplace will make up its own with help from texts, blogs, emails, and Facebook.

10. You don't control who trusts you. You only control the behavior that causes people to trust (or distrust) you.

1980, My XO Rick DeFatta and I, briefing a Senior Officer on a deployment to Germany.

QUESTIONS I GET ASKED

At the end of my 4-3-2-1 Leadership keynote talk, I open up the floor to questions. Some organizers seed the audience with example questions, other organizers ask individuals to create and pose their own questions, and at other times, I just flounder on my own until a question comes.

When I began giving speeches on leadership, I found this last part of my presentation to be the most stressful portion of any program, regardless of the audience. I have learned that patience and a willingness to tolerate silence for what feels like minutes (it's normally not more than 60 seconds) to be an effective generator of questions.

I'm not competing with David Letterman, who has had his "Top 10" lists for over 27 years. However, after over 100 presentations over the past 3+ years of speaking, here are the top 10 Questions I get asked and my answers:

(I own these answers. They are not Department of Defense or federal spin. They are how I think and feel.)

1. Should we still be in Iraq and/or Afghanistan?

In Afghanistan we went for the right reasons. Al Queda started there, planned the 9-11 attacks from there and believed they could operate from there in the future with impunity. We sadly took our eye off that priority and turned to Iraq. Now eleven years after 9-11, we have departed Iraq and are in the process of disengaging from leading combat operations in Afghanistan. Time will tell if our efforts will bear the fruit of some form of democracy. I believe it will take a generation to determine if we were successful or not. We cannot want peace and democracy for these nations more than their populations do. Our Soldiers, Sailors, Airmen, and Marines and a large number of civilian contractors made the ultimate sacrifice. Future operations in this era of global turmoil and conflict will require American support. It cannot, however, be only military solution sets that we bring to these problems. We must bring the full weight of our excellence and expertise to bear. From Agriculture, to Commerce, to Health and Human Services, to the Peace Corps, these will be the carriers of the message that America cares, and America must remain engaged in the world.

2. Tell us about a leadership mistake you made.

I am the perfect example that we are not a "Zero Defects" Army. I made the rank of Major General; however, I made more than my fair share of mistakes. I took other people's shares as well. One mistake really stands out because it hit me so unexpectedly and so very hard.

In the summer of 1993, I assumed command of the 701st. My direct superior had only relinquished command of the 701st just four years before I arrived (so he knew the Battalion). One of the Battalion's responsibilities was overseeing the dining facility for the 4,000 Soldiers of my superior's command (note: I said overseeing, not directing). This required us to coordinate the dining facility operations. It worked fairly well but it always was difficult. After a few months, I thought of a way out of this duty. I went to my superior's deputy and made him an offer. I'd give the responsibility of running the operation to the Logistics Officer on my boss's staff. To sweeten the deal, I would also give up one to two Officers to oversee the operation. The deputy, thankfully, decided to educate me: "Vinny, whenever an issue comes up with the other units, the boss listens. If it's about the 701st, all the boss ever says is, 'I didn't have that problem. What's Boles' problem?' I appreciate the offer, but you don't want to do this. You have to figure it out."

Properly chastened and warned, I went back to work. We had Thanksgiving in about 60 days, and Thanksgiving is a big deal. So I had meetings on a weekly basis. I gave guidance, inspected, and basically put all my excess energy into ensuring that Thanksgiving, 1993 was going to be a rip-roaring success. The night before Thanksgiving, I visited the kitchen and the dining hall to see how the prep was going. It was less than I expected, and I let my disappointment show to the cooks that were there.

The next day, about an hour before serving started, I returned to the Dining Hall and my jaw dropped. It was magnificent. The Mess Sergeant had released the majority of her cooks early the day before and had them come back at midnight to hit it hard and continuously. The place shone, there were platters, ice sculptures, and decorations galore. It looked like a restaurant preparing for the award of a Michelin Star. As I was still trying to get my head around what I was seeing, I noticed a civilian jazz band setting up in the corner. The Mess Sergeant arrived and as I was complimenting her, she stoically listened to me. Finally, I asked about the jazz band. Where had they come from? She informed me that the band members were friends with the cooks, and they agreed to play for a reduced fee. When I mentioned that no one had told me, she screwed up her courage, looked me in the eye and said, "We can have a good idea once in a while, too, Sir."

I learned a lesson. I had focused more of my attention on the pressure I was feeling from above than on my teammates below.

I committed then and there to take better care of those cooks and the team that ran the Dining Facility, and they repaid us by winning award after award, feeding Soldiers well in the field or at home station.

To this day one of my special memories is of that Mess Sergeant, two years later, having me present her Meritorious Service Medal when she departed. It showed I could learn, too.

3. **How do you handle a "bad" boss?**

Sometimes you can't; however, I have found that the same rule with poorly performing subordinates applies. That is, "Do not back them into a corner." Some superiors don't know they are "bad." They are doing what got them there and they may be, at least initially, in over their head in a new position. Be helpful. Suggest after-meetings, or in-private sessions, suggest alternatives to a course of action they are thinking of. Always be helpful.

4. Are there exceptions to this rule?

Yes. The exception is if the superior is doing anything that is illegal, immoral, unethical or unsafe. If you fail to stand up, then you become an accomplice. I am not naive. It is easy to say you will step up and say something, but much harder to do. But the situation will not get better with the absence of action. There are usually a number of agencies to turn to: OSHA, EEO, and many companies have hotlines or help lines, and there is always the media. This may entail you losing your job, but only you can answer the question, "How bad do I want to work here?" My answer: "If you want it bad enough, you'll get it bad enough."

5. Did you have someone you couldn't work with?

I did. I had an assignment where I had a civilian subordinate, entrenched in the job for many years, an expert in the subject area, who made every action a contest. Every request met with an incredulous look and the question "Why?" It was the longest two years I had. In retrospect I learned a great deal about behavior vs. personalities. I had to rise above the pettiness and be objective. For example, I asked, "What specifically was wrong about the request that was made?" You might ask, "Why didn't we just fire the person?" The person had built up a constituency, and my new boss did not want to upset that applecart in the workforce. So it fell to me to "Deal with it, Vinny." After the two years were up and I prepared to leave, my boss did move the person. Having seen my boss's patience with the employee's behavior, the workforce didn't want to put up with the employee anymore. You will always have some folks who test you. Don't get personal, be objective, document poor performance, and in time (longer than you might like, I admit), everything will sort out.

6. What is the Army's Leadership Secret?

The Army is almost 238 years old, older than the nation itself. In 2004 the Chief of Staff of the Army laid out the two Core Competencies for the US Army in the Army Posture Statement, which, I believe, remain valid today as they were in 1775.

- Train and equip Soldiers and grow leaders.

- Provide relevant and ready land power capability when and where needed.

Note the first competency—Train and Grow Leaders. We don't contract out for leadership. The Army grows its own, forged in the harshness of training, tested in combat and developed through rigorous professional development.

The essence of the Army I believe is found in its constancy. I have come to call it a "Values Based, Standards Driven" institution. Wherever I went in the Army, I knew what the values were (note that their first letters spell out the acronym "LDRSHIP").

Loyalty

Duty

Respect

Selfless Service

Honor

Integrity

Personal Courage

The "secret," if it is one, is that these values are what you cling to when challenges arise. If values are to have meaning, leaders can't throw them over the side when those values are tough to adhere to. Our Army is not a perfect institution. We can find examples in some of our challenges in the last decade that were in the news: the prison at Abu Ghraib, Walter Reed and its treatment of Wounded Warriors, the failure to correctly address the circumstances of Pat Tillman's death. These challenges were not caused by our values. Rather, each of these was caused when we deviated from those values.

So the secret is shared values and individuals committed to them up and down the organization.

7. How do you take care of yourself?

Like anyone else, taking care of myself gets harder as I get older, and I travel a bit. But a senior leader once told me that I had to do four things every day to stay fit: think, read, exercise, and get good sleep.

Thinking and reading come pretty easily to me and always have. Exercise is more of a challenge because as I get older, I am finding that things that stress me but don't hurt me seem to be the answer. So I do Hot Bikram Yoga three to four times per week and swim two or three times a week. This routine seems to keep me flexible, and the swimming works my muscles and cardio. Sleep has not usually been a problem except when I travel. Then the key is to hydrate and stay in a sleep routine (some light stretching and exercise before bedtime helps).

8. You talked in the previous question about reading. What do you recommend?

I just queried Amazon.com for leadership books and received 83,832 results, so it's a bit daunting to recommend THE BOOK on leadership. I do find biographies and autobiographies on leaders to be valuable as I reflect on the subject. A few I would recommend:

- Forest Pogue's series on George Marshall

- David Halberstam's book on the Korean War, *The Coldest Winter* (the best book to discuss the various levels of leadership—strategic, operational and tactical)

- Rick Atkinson's series on the U.S. Army in World War II. Volume I, *An Army at Dawn*, winner of the Pulitzer Prize, and Volume II, *The Day of Battle*, have been published, and Volume III is scheduled for publication in 2013.

- LTG® Hal Moore and Joe Galloway's book, *We Were Soldiers Once and Young*. It captures the stress of training, deployment, combat, and the actions of leaders on the battlefield. It has since been made into a film starring Mel Gibson.

I also read Fast Company and the Harvard Business Review to stay up to date on the business world.

Whatever you read, act on your curiosity and feed it. When I hear of something I don't know about, I reach for a book on the subject.

9. What are your thoughts on micromanagement?

I have been guilty of micromanagement on occasion. It usually occurs in two instances. First: If something interests my boss, then it absolutely fascinates me, and I want to ensure we are meeting the boss's standards. So I'll get involved up front and early and that can possibly be taken for micromanagement. Usually once I am sure we are meeting the standard, I ease off and allow the team to work it. Two exceptions were safety and my signature. If these are involved, I stay engaged and don't apologize for it. It does help the process if I explain my rationale so my team expects it and that explanation becomes routine. The second instance involves the subject of subordinate experience. If the team is experienced on the task, I back off. If they are inexperienced, I will engage until we build a routine to get a base of experience. I don't try to do their job. I work to ensure they know how to do their job. It also helps to have a trusted agent who can keep you grounded if you go overboard with this. Mine was usually my wife, Cheryl or one of the first-rate Command Sergeant Majors I had: CSM Cox, Tuxhorn, Erazo and Stewart always felt free to keep me honest in this regard.

Simply stated: When in doubt and your team is experienced, under-manage. When in doubt and your team is inexperienced, over-manage them.

10. Who has inspired you?

Army is a "team event." Solo performers don't get very far nor last very long. I had a lot of great teammates, great bosses, and superb subordinate Commanders who kept me straight and excused my shortcomings. I'm honored at the many who keep in touch still. The backbone of the Army, however, rests in the capable hands of its Non-commissioned Officers. Nothing happens in the Army until a Sergeant details Soldiers and resources to a task. Above them, it's concepts and orders. At their level is the decisive node.

Here are five whose fingerprints are all over those stars I was honored to wear as a General Officer, and they truly inspired me.

John Anderson

As a Captain at Fort Knox, Kentucky, I had John Anderson as my First Sergeant. An Irish immigrant, he often told the story of how he came to America on Thanksgiving and was in basic training by that Christmas. An outstanding mechanic, a master paratrooper, a selfless Sergeant, he was the best counselor a young Captain could have (and I needed him). His counsel in April 1981 kept me in the Army when I thought of resigning. He retired as the Maintenance Department Sergeant Major at the Armor School after 36+ years of military service, and he did not volunteer to leave.

Everett "Bud" Tuxhorn

At the 701st I received a Command Sergeant Major who was abusive and out of control. After attempts to counsel him failed to correct his behavior, he was relieved. Though we needed a replacement, none was available. "Bud" was a Command Sergeant Major in an Infantry Battalion and his unit had just had some promotions, so he was deemed available. He volunteered to leave the Infantry and come to a Support Battalion, and he was superb in every way. Respectful, calm, professional, and exceptional in working with young Officers, he epitomized the phrase, "He can step on your shoes and still leave a shine." He retired to Colorado and is engaged in the ministry. He honored me by asking me to be his best man.

Tomas Erazo Ramos

In 1997 I was a new Colonel and assigned to command the Support Command for the 4th Infantry Division at Fort Hood, Texas. With the post-Cold War drawdowns, there were shortages in the Officer ranks. To offset these shortages, Tomas stepped up and ensured our Sergeants did more than their fair share of the heavy lifting, and ensured our success in a number of high visibility fieldings and training operations. He asked only one thing of me—"That there is no seam between us." It was an easy promise to keep. Tomas is retired to Puerto Rico and teaches Junior ROTC. Retired but Still Serving.

CSM David Stewart

When I assumed command at Rock Island six weeks before the attacks of 9-11, David was my Command Sergeant Major. We were composed of 90% civilians and contractors. It would have been easy for him to just worry about the Soldiers. But he was the unit's Command Sergeant Major and he mentored, educated, and supported those civilians. I lost track of the times he would walk the halls of the headquarters or visit a unit in the field and come back with sage insights and advice: "Sir, you need to visit the data entry team. They are really kicking it and could use a lift." That insight was just one example of his value added. When I was ordered to deploy to Kuwait to prepare for Operation Iraqi Freedom, he was packing his bags before I said a word and he truly was a franchise player for me, the unit, and the nation.

David Wood

To say he was a stoic Soldier is putting it mildly. Born in Iran, he was adopted by an American family that worked in the oil fields in Southwest Asia. Our paths crossed when I assumed command of the 3rd COSCOM in Iraq in July 2003 during OIF 1. As I was going about the process of selecting him, I ran into an Officer who had served with him. When I inquired about him, the Officer was unambiguous. "Sir, I have two sons. If they went to combat with David Wood, he would ensure they were trained to the highest standards and before they died, he would..." (that was all I needed to hear). If ever a sergeant had my back, it was David Wood. He was everywhere, in everything and if a Sergeant was unsure what to do, he only had to watch and model David Wood. He is still on active duty and still making a difference.

I was a fortunate Officer. With leaders like these taking care of me, it was easier to succeed. They made failure unacceptable by making it too difficult to go there. I am in their debt, then, now, and forever. They made me a better Officer, Commander, and leader.

THOUGHTS TO LEAVE YOU WITH

"There is no real ending. It's just the place where you stop the story."

— Frank Herbert

A t this point in my presentation, having taken the audience's questions, I have to, as Herbert says above, "stop the story." I close the event with a section titled "Thoughts to Leave You With" during which I share anecdotes that, having researched the audience, I believe will provide a great closing to highlight the message and their theme. Here are five to which, over time, I have received the most positive response from audiences.

Ask More - Tell Less: Leaders Take Excuses Away

The higher in rank I went, the more I realized that I had perspective and experience but it is the people on the ground, closest to the action, that usually (almost always) have the most relevant information. So I don't focus on having the "answers" when they come to me for approval of an action; rather I focus on asking the questions that will expose a blind spot or identify a stakeholder that has been missed and will be critical to the effort. One area this has been helpful was when my subordinate units were planning training events. When units plan training they will "overfill" the calendar, literally trying to cram multiple events into a time slot that will really support only one or two. This is because they want to get the training in but overestimate the capability of the students to assimilate the training. My role there is usually to offer a "training appetite suppressant." We'll work to identify the most critical training and highlight that. I have found troops appreciate getting the time to get a few tasks done to standard vs. the fire hose approach.

I didn't come to this revelation on my own. I had a General Officer, General Jerry Rutherford, who would listen to us brief and if he heard something that didn't pass his common sense meter he wouldn't say "no." Rather, he would ask, "Tell me how you thought your way through that?" It never failed. As we would wax on about our innovative approach, or new technique, he would intently listen and tactfully offer a question or two that usually brought us back to the ground.

This technique served me very well as a General Officer, where I would have any number of subject mater experts who were more informed than I would ever be. They did need my approval and I'd go through the read-ahead packet and have my questions ready. The only capability you need for this to work is to truly believe that there are no "stupid questions." If they had the answers, their and my confidence would rise. If they didn't, they usually did some research and learned something.

Another aspect as I got more senior was to use my position and influence to take excuses away. If something that had to get done wasn't going well, it normally usually wasn't for lack of desire or effort. Something above my folk's pay grade was getting in the way. My job was to find it and adjust it so they could be successful. It might entail providing new guidance to adjust the task standard or getting to someone on the staff and free up an action that was needed so the folks on the ground could execute what I wanted, to name just a few.

Often just asking the questions, "How can I help you?" or "What help do you need?" would identify excuses I could go to work on.

Bottom line, as you go higher up the chain you will know fewer details but have more experience and judgment. Your team will usually know what's needed, especially if you ask them "What would you do?" After they get over the surprise, they will think a bit and provide an insight that you, as the leader, didn't have.

Don't worry, if you picked the right folks and asked the right questions, you rarely have to dictate the solution.

You Don't Get to Choose Your Missions

When a task came my way, I very rarely got a vote if I wanted to do it or not. It was either something our unit was expected to do because we had the capability, or it was something that needed to get done and it had been decided that we had to do it. The mission was usually accompanied by these statements: "You're the only ones available" or "The boss wants you to do this one."

What you do control is your mindset, your attitude toward the task. As a leader, if your reaction is "This isn't fair" or "We're getting hosed," then you are going to infect your team with a negative attitude, which doesn't do anyone any good. This is especially the case when the mission is a short-fused or high-visibility one. These pressures just add to the burden. I have seen units get a task on a Wednesday, complain about it for two days and on Friday afternoon they still had to do it anyway, but now they just have less time. I have found it's better to grab the task and get after it with a positive attitude rather than complain. Your boss probably knows you'll get the task done and that it's not completely fair, and the boss will appreciate not having to be reminded that the tasking was a less than optimum piece of scheduling by his or her staff.

Let me be clear. I am not saying you roll over for every short-fused mission and act like Pollyanna no matter how unfair the task. If you get an extremely unfair mission, then after the mission is done, you need to see the powers that be and lay out the view from your desk, foxhole, or vehicle and highlight your concerns and get them addressed.

I have found that you can wear out the "go to people" by going to them too often. Staffs, relieved that they have this "go to" capability forget that. They think they can just turn to those folks and they'll be there.

In March of 1991 during Operation Desert Shield/Desert Storm, our unit, the 3rd Brigade of the 2nd Armored Division had crossed into Iraq. We expected fierce resistance, however, once we saw the effects of the bombing and artillery campaigns we saw the opportunity to quickly move. My responsibility was to manage the supply stocks, making sure they were where they needed to be, when they needed to be there. Our standard operating procedure (SOP) was to carry three days of supplies with us. In combat the most critical supplies for an armored force (M1 tanks, M2 Bradley fighting vehicles, heavy tracked artillery) are fuel (do not want to stop) and ammunition (can't fight without it). We were fine on fuel stocks, however, we only had enough ammunition on the systems for three days, not for a burst across the desert. We had to go back into Saudi Arabia, link up with our ammunition stocks (thankfully uploaded on trucks) and bring them forward for this revised offensive. To issue ammunition for an armored force, you need forklifts that aren't suited for a warehouse floor but can operate in sand and other difficult terrain. We had the ones we needed, rough terrain forklifts. Our SOP was to put them on a trailer, bring them forward to the ammunition points and download them, so they could move the heavy weights of the ammunition stockpiles quickly. We needed to put them on trailers because just like a civilian warehouse forklift, rough terrain forklifts are not designed for a drive down the highway. They are meant to be a workhorse, not a thoroughbred. We were out of trailers, but I had a phenomenal ammunition team, ably led by a great technical expert, Chief Warrant Officer Bob Woodham. From the time he received these forklifts he maintained them, trained his people on them and took care of the machines.

I drove back into the ammo point in Saudi Arabia and informed Bob of the change in our mission. We were to move out and link up with the 3rd Brigade in Iraq. "How far do we have to go?" he asked.

"We'll know when we find them" was the best answer I could give.

In training his team on the forklifts, Bob had discovered the machines could be driven if we raised the forks way up in the air above the vehicle. That method seemed to work, and Bob's team did not want to view the fight from the back bench. So off we went, 30+ ammunition trucks, fuel trucks and six rough terrain forklifts across the desert, no highways, no lights, no 7-11 rest stops, no Holiday Inns. We averaged about 15 miles an hour because that was about as fast as the forklifts could go and still be operational when we got to our destination and had to employ them to issue ammunition. We left about noon, as I recall. It was the longest night of my life, and those Soldiers and their equipment didn't falter. That night, those workhorses performed like thoroughbreds.

The 3rd Brigade meanwhile had been very successful in their offensive maneuver. We found them in Kuwait 18 hours later (back then without Mapquest, I figured it at about 225+ miles). They had raced across Iraq, defeating anything that got in their way and were guided to Kuwait by the glow of the burning oil wells Saddam Hussein's forces had ignited.

Early the next morning our Brigade Commander saw the ammunition trucks in Kuwait and asked my boss where they had come from. He just pointed to me and informed him I had gone to get them, making it sound effortless. I can still see, even 20 years later, the incredulous look on the Brigade Commander's face when he heard that news.

That "go to" ammunition team was there for me, and once again, I had a valuable lesson reinforced. Manuals and the SOPs have to be viewed as a start point to move from. The technical manual for the forklift didn't have a section on driving across the desert for 18+ hours. Our SOP hadn't factored in operating without trailers. But I had a team that factored in that they could do it. Manuals and SOPs don't account for leadership and attitude— leaders do.

Your Three Qualities

While I was at Fort Hood as a Brigade Commander, I was responsible for a unit whose mission and capabilities I was not familiar with. This unit was an aviation maintenance unit, and their Commander was a very competent and stoic Officer from whom I learned a great deal about aviation logistics. We had very different personalities, which brought some challenges to our relationship. We parted ways on good terms and nine years later, we crossed paths again in the Pentagon. He had since retired and was on the staff in another section of the Pentagon, and I was the Deputy for the Army Logistics Staff. We would meet in the hallways, cross-talk, share a smile and a story, and move on.

One day, one of his subordinates let us know that my aviation logistics Commander's father had passed away and would be interred at Arlington

National Cemetery. My staff discovered the date and time and I went to the internment. People who wish to attend an internment gather at a building at the cemetery in a designated room. Once everyone is there, the cemetery staff ensures linking up the chaplain, the burial detail and attendees together for a drive to the gravesite and the internment. As we were waiting, the family reflected on the father. He was a career Soldier, served in multiple wars, had a long and successful marriage with great sons and family—all in all, a life fully and well lived in the service of others.

At this point, the chaplain stepped forward to the deceased's wife and said, "I didn't know your husband. In order to help me make my remarks at the gravesite, could you tell me three qualities that made him unique?"

That hit me. All that life and we were asked to sum it up in three words. The chaplain's request made me think: What would my three words be? Would I know what those three words were and if I did, would I be proud of them? Would the three qualities named by my family be the same as the three qualities named by my work colleagues?

What are your three qualities? Do you know them? Would you be proud of them? Would they be consistent between your family and work life?

The people you come in contact with already judge what those three qualities are now. You can work on those qualities now or cross your fingers and wait until your gravesite service and see what everyone comes up with. I don't know about you, but I'm not waiting.

That day at Arlington, the family named their father's three qualities. As I recall, they were the following: He was tough, he worked very hard, and he had a great sense of humor.

I'd take those.

When Do You Smile?

I was at a ceremony for a Colonel who was being promoted to Brigadier (One-Star) General. He began to tell a story about a young girl in a Swiss orphanage in the 1950's. She had come to the orphanage because she was a single mother from Austria and did not want to have the child in her hometown. After her delivery, she returned to Austria asking the nuns at the orphanage to try to find an American family for her child. The nuns listened but there were no guarantees.

At about the same time, a U.S. Army Communications Sergeant in Europe was talking with his wife one evening. She was finally getting him to accept that she would be unable to bear any children. After discussing this, the couple decided to approach the local priest and seek his guidance. The priest informed the couple that he knew of an orphanage in Switzerland. Arrangements were made and an appointment was scheduled. This was not only significant for the couple but also the orphanage; if the orphanage could make an inroad with this couple, it might help many other babies looking for parents as well.

In true military fashion, baby cribs were arrayed in a line and the prospective mom could, in effect, "troop the line" and see if there was a child she felt a connection with. Midway down the line, the woman stopped and looking at the nuns, she said, "That baby smiled at me. That looks like a happy baby."

At this point in the ceremony, our newest Brigadier General commented, "I didn't know how big a deal it was to smile, but I'm damn sure glad I smiled that day."

When do you smile? Do you realize that the cues you give off can be a powerful incentive or disincentive to your teammates? You will probably spend more time with these teammates than with your family. If you are walking around with a "poor me" attitude, complaining about your being overworked and underappreciated, coming in early, staying late and moaning about it the whole time, then rest assured, the folks working for you aren't aspiring for a career in your image. They will count the days until you leave or look for alternative employment options.

I have discovered few interactive tools as powerful and immediately effective as a smile on a person that I'm working with and few as demoralizing as the gloomy Gus who sucks the joy and energy out of the room and the people in it.

If your team is down, what are you doing to cause that attitude? And what are you doing to fix it?

I've Got Bad News and Good News

First, the bad news: Leading people is *hard* work. It requires consistency of action and persistency of effort. You can't tell your team that your "good" leadership days are only on Monday-Wednesday and Friday, and if they need your leadership on Tuesday or Thursday, well, too bad. You have to be the leader when they need you, whoever "they" are in whatever capacity "they" need you. There is no leadership "off" switch, and I have seen this lack of an "off" switch become even more pronounced in the more connected digital world that we find ourselves in today. No matter that it's evening for you; it's a workday for someone on the other side of the world and that person isn't going to use snail mail to obtain a leadership solution. That person is going to want you now.

Now, the good news: Leading people is *not complicated*. It doesn't require a PhD to be an effective leader. Look at the concepts you have been exposed to in this book.

Nothing here is groundbreaking. In fact, I have finished this presentation and had audience members inform me that they didn't hear anything new. But when I ask, "So was it valuable?" the answer is unfailingly "Yes." Then I pursue for a little deeper understanding. "What was really helpful?" I ask. "You gave me a new and simpler way to think about leadership, and I can put your handout under my desk glass and begin using the tips on it right away."

That was the idea in building this presentation in 2004 at the training base. People just wanted tools. They had the motivation, the desire. They wanted more tools to practice and to be more effective at the craft and artistry of leadership.

I use the word "craft" because when I see really competent craftspeople, regardless of the craft (cooking, auto repair, carpentry, plumbing, bricklaying, or anything requiring competence and the knowledge of the critical details to pay attention to), those people know what to do, what exact tool to use (I need a 5/8 not a 7/8 wrench) to get the exact effect the task requires. When it's well done, leadership is a craft and when it's done superbly, it's an art.

I can borrow the words of St. Francis of Assisi to express this idea in another way: "He who works with his hands is a laborer. He who works with his hands and his head is a craftsman. He who works with his hands and his head and his heart is an artist." Bring your hands, head, and heart into every leadership equation you are attempting to solve.

If you are a leader who works hard to establish structure, manage your relationships, balance risks, and make decisions; if you ask and answer the three critical questions for your team; if you address the causes of stress and focus your efforts on establishing and maintaining trust, you cannot help but be successful.

Enjoy the journey.

2001, Memorial Day in my hometown Bronxville, NY
with my Goddaughter Kelly Maureen.

AFTERWORD
America's Sons and Daughters
in Uniform Weren't My Only Teachers

When most people read "What America's Sons and Daughters Taught Me" in the title of this book, they probably assume I am referring to the Soldiers and civilians I trained with, deployed with, and served with. These Soldiers and civilians made me their "training aid," so I could learn from them on this leadership journey of over 33 years. However, these folks weren't my only teachers. You never know where the lessons will come from. Mine came from a second-grade class at Our Lady of Lourdes School in Bettendorf, Iowa.

My deputy at the Field Support Command was a career civil servant named Ron Herter. Ron is indicative of the term "quiet professional." A career civil servant since his graduation from Penn State with his concentration in Logistics, Ron had it all; calm, exceptionally competent and perceptive, he was the perfect "yin" to my "yang." I always benefitted from asking him, "What am I missing?" Sometimes he had an answer on the spot; sometimes, he would excuse himself and go circulate through the "cubicle farm" at the headquarters, make a few phone calls (he never used email to make these inquiries), and when he returned, I had a more complete picture. On occasion, Ron's inquiries confirmed what I knew or thought I knew, and other times, his work revealed a blind spot.

Because Ron was so quiet, he was a bit reserved, and after having been at Field Support Command for a year, I was just beginning to get to know Ron beyond the work environment. In September 2002, Ron came into my office and in a slow and low voice, he said, "Barbara wants me to ask you if you would do something." October was National Reading Month, and Barbara, Ron's wife, wanted to know if I would be a celebrity reader at her school, Our Lady of Lourdes in Bettendorf, Iowa. I agreed and looked forward to the event.

On the day I was scheduled to attend Barbara's school, I held one of my monthly Town Hall forums for the Field Support Command team. One of the challenges since 9-11 was keeping folks informed and being open to questions and their concerns in this ever-changing conflict. By the fall of 2002, we mistakenly thought we had "Victory" in Afghanistan, and the FSC team was turning their efforts toward supporting whatever operations would unfold in Iraq. To keep the team at headquarters informed, I usually held a monthly Town Hall forum, which was a combination hail and fare-well (say hello to new folks and farewell to departing folks), an awards ceremony for employees or teams of employees who had distinguished themselves, a birthday recognition, and finally, an update from me on recent and upcoming events. I always opened these Town Hall meetings to questions, and I did not have a bashful bunch. They were pretty up front with me. We had been through a lot together in a fast and furious year since the 9-11 attacks.

On that October day in 2002, I decided to turn the tables on the FSC by starting off with my own question. "Let me ask you all something," I said to the over 70 employees and Soldiers in the group. "I have to go to Our Lady of Lourdes School tonight to read to the children. What uniform should I wear that would make an impression on the children? Should I wear my Battle Dress Uniform (BDUs), or should I wear the dress uniform with my stars and ribbons?" (I was leaning toward the dress uniform.)

Their answer was immediate, unanimous, and it came at me like a tidal wave. "The BDUs," they shouted. I asked why and one of the employees informed me, "The BDUs are what kids want to wear when they think of Soldiers. If you wear the dress uniform, you'll look like a bus driver."

So that night, in my BDUs, I headed off with Cheryl to Lourdes. By that time, I had 27 years in the Army, and after all the moves and arriving at new locations, you can't help but pick up a "sixth sense" when you walk into some place for the first time. You get a first impression, informed by your experiences. And what a first impression Our Lady of Lourdes School made on me. The Church in general and the Iowa archdiocese were having difficulties coping with the unfolding scandals with priests and students. But Barbara Herter and her staff, their school untainted by scandal, were taking care of their part of the Catholic tradition.

The positive energy was palpable, upbeat, and infectious. I went into the assembly hall and met my new "battle buddies," my fellow readers for the evening: the Bettendorf Police Chief, a player from the local semi-pro hockey team (the Quad City Mallards), and a local artist. After being introduced to the students and parents, we were each given a teacher to escort us to a room to read the story to multiple classes that would rotate through during the evening. And then it happened; I was touched by Vinnie Smith's second-grade class.

"Vinnie" (her given name is Lavinda) was about 5'2" tall and 99 pounds after a full meal and a soaking with her clothes on. Her size was irrelevant; her professional bearing and attention to detail in a classroom were the equal of any drill sergeant (she missed nothing). In terms of energy, she made me look like a dim bulb (and this was in the evening after she had taught for a full day). As she looked me up and down, I could tell I was being measured. Being very gracious, she escorted me into her classroom, showed me around and then said, "OK, General. Here's the book and here come the children." And off I went to my assigned seat. My story was "Topsy Turvy Kingdom" and as the students settled in on the floor, I noticed every parent in the back of the room was measuring the General as well.

The reading went great, and I especially enjoyed the questions: "Why do you tuck your laces into your boot tops?" (So they won't catch on shrubs or branches and hold you up when you are on the move.) "Do you have a dog?" (Yes, and her name is Sweetie.) "Are you afraid when you have to go to war?" (You are concerned, but the key is not to let fear overcome you. And the key to not letting fear overcome you is being a great teammate for your team.)

Another group came in, the cycle repeated itself, and the second reading was as much fun as the previous one. After a reception and more meeting with parents, Cheryl and I headed home. Both products of Catholic schools, Cheryl and I reflected on our visit on the drive home, and we agreed that our experience at Our Lady of Lourdes School was unlike any other school experience we had been associated with. Whatever the school lacked in resources was more than supplanted by the love and positive energy wrapped around those children.

The next day, I wrote Barbara and Vinnie thank-you notes and sent a small contribution. When Barbara called to thank me for the contribution, I told her I didn't think of it as a gift. Rather, I saw myself as an investor in the future, and the Lourdes team looked like a pretty good one to bet on.

The next month, I went off on a whirlwind tour of Kuwait, Qatar, and Europe. My aide, Lt. Cassandra Avery, and I were discussing the trip and came up with the idea to send postcards to Vinnie's class while we traveled. Upon our return to the States, we were greeted in the headquarters with a massive thank-you note from Vinnie's class and an invitation to participate in the mass to honor the feast of St. Lucia. I thought that the children would just be attending the mass, and I would sit with them. Instead, these second-graders were running the mass. They were lectors for the scriptures, sang in the choir, brought up the offerings, acted as altar servers, sat with Cassandra and me, and directed us where to be and when during the mass.

The second-graders' enthusiasm reinforced my sense of how special a group of children these young treasures were.

A few weeks later during the unit's Christmas party, the employees all gathered for a luncheon and the usual gift-giving exchange. Imagine my surprise when I saw the Our Lady of Lourdes School's choir arrive as our special entertainment with Vinnie's big smile and a look in her eyes that said, "Are you surprised now, General Boles?" The choir was the hit of the party (even when they let me join them singing).

Between the party and Christmas, I received confirmation that I would deploy shortly after New Years Day to Kuwait and would prepare the supplies and equipment for issue to the forces readying for the invasion into Iraq. My return date was open-ended—I'd be back when the Army told me to go back.

Though Cheryl and I had experience with deployments, I came to realize how emotional this move was for the unit and the surrounding community. This was their first deployment. At the New Years' reception at our quarters, the wishes were especially heartfelt and the hugs especially long. People shook Cheryl's hand and inquired, "Are you going to be OK?"

What normally happens next after a spouse deploys is that the home-bound spouse gets the well-intentioned offer of "Call us if you need anything." Most spouses, however, not wanting to be a burden, suck it up and press on.

Not Our Lady of Lourdes—the folks at that school weren't about to leave Cheryl on her own.

Every day, Barbara called Cheryl with a quick "Thinking of you" or "How are you?" or "Can we stop by?" (They just "happened" to be in the neighborhood.) Every week, Vinnie Smith invited Cheryl to the class to be a reading tutor. Every weekend, Barbara and Ron called and took Cheryl to dinner or invited her for pizza and a movie at their house.

In Kuwait, Lt. Avery brought a box into my office. The box contained over a hundred letters from the Lourdes' students. My second-graders had organized a letter writing campaign to "Any Soldier." One night, we posted the letters all around the "cubicle farm" that we called the office area. Soldiers and staff teams began to write back. I became known as the "General the kids write to."

On their last school day of 2003, I was invited to call into Lourdes for the pledge of allegiance. It was a special end to a unique and treasured year-long experience (or so I thought).

In June 2003, after the initial invasion and we realized that this would not be another "100 Hour War" like Desert Shield/Desert Storm, I was notified to get back to Rock Island, move Cheryl and me to Europe, and then deploy to Balad, Iraq to assume command of the 3rd Corps Support Command (COSCOM). I'd come back when the Army told me to (the 3rd COSCOM's home base was Wiesbaden, Germany).

On 23 June, I arrived back home and then met the flurry of events that accompany a change of command: performance reports to close out, farewell dinners, packers (What comes to Europe? What goes in storage?), what airline can Sweetie (a 13-year-old Labrador) fly on in the summer? The change of command was set for 2 July, and our departure to Germany was scheduled for 21 July.

Knowing how special my relationship with the Lourdes' children was, Cheryl reached out to Barbara and Vinnie. Even though the change-of-command ceremony took place after school let out, twelve of the 16 newly promoted second-graders and their parents rearranged their schedules to attend the ceremony. They sat right behind Cheryl and my mom. Every one of those kids wore a way-too-large white T-shirt that had the kid's name and a stick figure on the front. Written above each stick figure were the words, "The General's Kids."

As I stood in the receiving line after the change-of-command ceremony, the children and Vinnie surprised me with a box. I opened it to find my T-shirt. On it were 16 named stick figures lined up under the words, "The General's Kids."

I promised those 16 kids that day that I would be back for their graduation, and in May 2009, in one of my last acts on active duty, I was the graduation speaker for those eighth-graders.

The local Quad Cities press has followed our friendship, and I learned that this generation is going to be fine. They will provide us no fewer challenges than my generation provided our elders, but I doubt my elders were as pleased with my result as I am with those young treasures from Lourdes.

With any luck, the legacy of leadership lives on, and this class will reach out and touch those who cross their future. That second-grade class from Our Lady of Lourdes School sure touched my life and Cheryl's in a way we needed, yet had not expected.

With every good wish for your future success and the prayer that this book inspires you to touch others as we have been touched.

May 2004, throwing out the first pitch at Yankee
Stadium after deployment. I can hear my staff saying,
"Don't bounce it in, Sir, get it over the plate!" (I did.)

ACKNOWLEDGMENTS

Just as an Army career is not a solo sport, neither is writing a book about it. I am indebted to all who made making my "best get better" part of their charge.

So much is owed to those who saw more potential in me than I ever considered: General Scott Wallace, General John Coburn, General Tom Metz, General Jerry Rutherford ("Someday you'll be a Battalion Commander, Vinny"), Colonel Steve Marshman, Colonel Bill Kearney and his son Lieutenant Colonel John Kearney, Major Ed Hart, and Gerry and Tori Tabin — they have kept the 701st family connected for almost 20 years after we left Fort Riley.

I have discovered that people hire speakers for two reasons: they have heard the speaker, or they trust someone who recommends the speaker. Special thanks to Mike Abrashoff and Tony D'Amelio who linked me to Harry Rhoads and the special team at the Washington Speakers Bureau — they are the "gold standard" in this business for a reason; they make my events look effortless, and they continue to recommend me to audiences. All I can say is, "Keep 'em coming."

My mother, Rita, was my first role model of selfless service and she still is. My three brothers, Kiernan, James, and Kevin, continue to ensure I don't take myself too seriously.

In pulling this book together, special thanks to Lari Bishop at Greenleaf Book Group. She took my first effort, put it aside and said, "Anyone can write the "A-Z leadership book.... Where is the 4-3-2-1 book?"

To Kent Gustavson, my publisher at Blooming Twig Books, and my editor, Sandra Shattuck, their patience and persistence brought this out of me, and it wouldn't have happened without them. They are the best, and they think I have more books in me; time will tell ...

Finally, to all the Soldiers who passed my way, they go into the dirt and the dark for us, to defend our Constitution and our way of life. All I would ask is that we be the type of citizens worthy of their service and sacrifice. I am a better person and Soldier for serving with them.

ABOUT THE AUTHOR

Retired Major General Vincent E. Boles is a speaker, trainer, and leader who has done more than read a textbook on the subject of leadership and logistics. He is a career Army Officer with 33 years of experience in staying ready for war and, when needed, leading teams into that war. Highlights from his experience in nine years as a General include the following:

- Managing the nation's $27 billion ammunition account.

- Assuming command of the Army's War Reserve equipment six weeks before the attacks of 9-11 and flexing it into operations in Afghanistan, Iraq and other locations.

- Deployed to Kuwait in preparation for the Invasion of Iraq with 142 personnel, which, in 90 days, grew to a force of over 8,000 Soldiers, Civilians and Contractors by the time the invasion began.

- Forward deployed from Kuwait into Iraq, he assumed command of the 16,000 personnel responsible for providing all logistical support and services to the 150,000 members of the coalition.

- Upon redeployment from combat operations, Vinny was assigned as the Army's 33rd Chief of Ordnance. Responsible for the doctrine, training, and professional excellence of the 120,000 Soldiers affiliated with the Corps, he made his primary focus taking the lessons learned in combat operations and embedding them in training programs.

Vinny is the President of Vincent E. Boles, Inc., a Leadership and Logistics consulting practice. He regularly speaks to corporate and association audiences, working to help individuals and teams ensure their "best gets better." To hire Vinny to speak to your group, contact him at www.vinnyboles.com.

YOUR NOTES PAGES

YOUR NOTES PAGES

YOUR NOTES PAGES

YOUR NOTES PAGES

YOUR NOTES PAGES

YOUR NOTES PAGES

YOUR NOTES PAGES